winning soccer

AL MILLER with Norm Wingert

Henry Regnery Company · Chicago

Library of Congress Cataloging in Publication Data

Miller, Al, 1936-
  Winning soccer.

  1. Soccer. I. Wingert, Norm, 1950-   joint
author. II. Title.
GV943.M55   796.33'42   74-27822
ISBN 0-8092-8308-5
ISBN 0-8092-8307-7 pbk.

My thanks to Dettmar Cramer and the United States Soccer
Federation Coaching School for many refreshing ideas on the game
of soccer; and to the Philadelphia Atoms staff, particularly Susan
Caulfield, for help in typing and preparing pictures and text.

Photographs by Newspix, Lansdowne, Pennsylvania

Published by Henry Regnery Company
  180 North Michigan Avenue, Chicago, Illinois 60601
Manufactured in the United States of America
Library of Congress Catalog Card Number: 74-27822
International Standard Book Number: 0-8092-8308-5 (cloth)
                                    0-8092-8307-7 (paper)

Published simultaneously in Canada by
Fitzhenry & Whiteside Limited
150 Lesmill Road
Don Mills, Ontario M3B 2T5
Canada

contents

Al Miller looks on with concern at
a tight moment for his team.

introduction

Soccer originated in very ancient times. There is evidence that a
primitive form of the game was played in China as early as 500 B.C.
And, in Europe, two tribes or communities of men kicked a skull
back and forth between their villages in the early centuries A.D.

England is credited with developing modern soccer, one impetus
being the use of a pig's bladder as a ball. In the 1200s, the game
had become so popular among the masses that King Edward banned
it, feeling that it was creating disorder among his subjects. But
the prohibition inspired rather than discouraged the game's
devotees, and soccer continued to be played.

Later, soccer repaid this debt of loyalty when it became the reason behind a new working class freedom—a half day of work on Saturdays. Because of rigid religious laws, soccer could not be played in England on Sunday. This left Saturday afternoon as the only feasible time for people to watch their teams perform. The government eventually made this half-day break official.

In 1863, formal rules for the game of "football" were established when the London Football Association met. They decided to call their brand of ball association football; the game's modern name, soccer, was eventually derived from "association." The laws of play, which refined the game, have remained basically the same since 1863. The number of players was reduced from former multitudes to 11; minimum and maximum field size were determined; and fouls and other misconduct were defined.

PRESENT

Today, soccer is played all over the world. Every country has a football or soccer association to govern the sport within the country. And these organizations all belong to the Federation Internationale de Football Association (FIFA), which is soccer's governing body worldwide.

The World Cup is one of the most sought-after team championships in the world. One hundred and forty-one countries vie for this coveted cup every four years. It is deemed so valuable, in fact, that winners become national heroes and losers earn national disgrace. One year, during qualifying matches between Honduras and El Salvador, a war was started over this prize. And, when Brazil won the World Cup in 1970, the country celebrated for two weeks, and all the players' earnings were declared tax-exempt by the president. (The most publicized and highly paid athlete in the world, Pele, played on this Brazilian team.) The World Cup was won by West Germany in 1974.

THE UNITED STATES AND SOCCER

Until recently, soccer has not flourished to the same degree in the

United States as in other countries. Though the well-known game in 1869 between Princeton and Rutgers was most certainly a soccer game, it gave rise first to rugby and later to football, rather than developing into modern soccer as early kicking games did elsewhere.

Amateur Soccer

For many years, in fact, soccer was played in the United States primarily by ethnic groups, who brought the game with them when they came to this country from abroad. And ethnic groups, today, continue to field teams in amateur soccer leagues. My first amateur team was a German club in Reading, Pennsylvania. Most of the players were immigrants, and a few other Americans and myself profited immensely from being exposed to them. I learned to dribble and control the ball with my feet; I experienced the exhilaration of scoring a goal and found satisfaction in teamwork and competition. It was a better brand of soccer, and, partly as a result of being exposed to it, I went on to play in high school and was motivated to go to college. There, my involvement with the game continued and deepened.

In recent years, the game of soccer in the United States has made great strides. Soccer's governing body in this country is the United States Soccer Federation (USSF) (admitted to FIFA in 1914), whose offices are located in the Empire State Building in New York City. Most states have a state association for soccer, which falls under USSF's jurisdiction. Thousands of volunteer hours are spent each year in administering, coaching, and managing amateur soccer in the United States. The youth leagues have grown so rapidly that it is nearly impossible to supply them with enough administrators, coaches, and referees. California, Seattle, Dallas, Long Island, and Philadelphia are among the cities that have had an unbelievable youth soccer development in the past five years.

America is still far behind many European and South American countries in development. But the day is coming when the United States will field a team worthy of the Olympic Gold Medal and the World Cup challenge.

Professional Soccer

Professional soccer in the United States has also been growing in leaps and bounds. It got its real start in the summer of 1967, just one year after the 1966 World Cup tournament in England. There, wealthy sports promoters saw soccer's potential when they observed the large and enthusiastic crowds.

The first attempt at professional organization went awry. Two leagues were formed at the same time and lost millions of dollars in their attempts to outdo each other. Out of this financial disaster, however, the North American Soccer League (NASL) arose. It floundered for awhile, but when Phil Woosnam, a dynamic man and tireless worker, became commissioner, it began to develop healthily. Today the NASL has teams all across the United States and Canada, and it is moving into the major sports scene at a rapid rate.

MY PERSONAL INVOLVEMENT

I have been fortunate in being able to watch and participate in this immense growth. As a player and coach I have been affiliated with every possible group in soccer circles. During college, I spent the winters, springs, and summers playing for amateur teams, and, as a professional, I have made countless friends, traveled extensively, and have found the most rewarding profession imaginable—coaching.

I have coached young boys, high school boys, college boys, and professional "boys." I say "boys" because, no matter how fiercely contested, the game of soccer is always fun for the players. It continues to intrigue me that, even after grueling practice sessions, players remain on the field, shooting at the goal or playing around with the ball. The soccer ball is magic; the joy of manipulating it with feet and head is an exhilarating experience.

I have also had the privilege of watching the game grow and develop. When I was playing, only the forwards were allowed to score goals; the rest of the players were strictly defenders. Today, that is no longer true; every player has opportunities to score. As a result, modern players are more skillful and versatile.

In the following pages, many ideas and practices used to develop top-flight players are presented. Some of these techniques are used all over the world; others, I have found to be personally effective.

However, it is important to remember that your development into a better player will take many hours of practice and concentration. Play at every opportunity you get—whether against a friend in the backyard or in a regulation game. Every soccer experience will improve your understanding of the game and your mastery of soccer techniques.

chapter one

tools of the trade

As in every other sport, good equipment is essential. Since soccer requires only a few pieces of clothing and a ball, it is a relatively inexpensive sport. However, this in no way means that you should purchase cheap equipment. A properly fitting uniform, a high quality ball—and above all else—well-fitting shoes are important if you are to turn in your best performance.

CLOTHING

Soccer Shirt

The soccer shirts worn by professionals are generally made of some form of nylon knit or lightweight cotton—long sleeved in winter, short sleeved in summer. It is most important that the neck not be tight, as your breathing may be hindered.

The shirt also has the player's identifying number on the back, and it must be large enough for the referee and spectators to see clearly. In the NASL, uniforms must have a 3-inch-high number on the front and the player's name on the back for television purposes.

In the past, when each soccer player on a team had a clearly defined role, his number corresponded with the position he played. The goalkeeper was assigned number 1, the right fullback number 2, and so on, right through the lineup to the left wing, who wore number 11. Today, however, with each player being called upon to assist his team in many ways, the old numbering system has lost meaning and has been discarded. Only the goalkeeper still sports his traditional number 1.

Soccer shirt

Shorts

Shorts should fit loosely around the legs to provide free movement in kicking and running. The waistband should not be tight since it might hinder your breathing. The best shorts are made of nylon, which is durable and lightweight.

Uniform Colors

Since a team is identified by its uniforms, uniform colors are chosen carefully with an eye to visibility and contrast. Not only do spectators recognize a team by its uniforms, but, in the confusion of rapid play, players use this distinguishing feature to find each other. Therefore, it is essential for the uniforms of players from different teams to contrast radically (i.e., if the home team wears dark shirts

Soccer shorts

and stockings, their opponents must wear white or light shirts and stockings).

Generally, team members wear their dominant color at home. Vertical and horizontal stripes are quite popular today, but plain shirts, also, are still in style. The referee wears black so that no passes are directed towards him.

Shoes

Shoes are the player's most important piece of equipment, because his feet are his most important consideration. It is essential that a player's shoes fit properly. Most players get shoes one-half size smaller than their regular street shoes. Good leather shoes tend to stretch as they break in, and, if the shoe becomes loose fitting, it tends to impede ball control and running.

Players for the Atoms wear one of three types of shoe—flat-soled, molded rubber, or studded—depending on the playing surface and playing conditions.

The flat-soled shoe is used exclusively for training. These shoes are very comfortable and are good for Astroturf practices. However, I do not advocate them for games, because the shoe is thin, and a player can get unnecessary bruises on his feet. The small molded-rubber shoe is used for playing on Astroturf, frozen fields, and hard ground. It has 14 small rubber studs on the sole rather than the six nylon studs that traditional, studded shoes have. These

Flat-soled shoe used for training purposes only, as it is too thin to afford the necessary protection in a game situation.

small studs provide traction, and the larger number of them increases shock absorption on hard surfaces. This shoe, developed just recently, is probably the most popular soccer shoe in America. Since the Atoms play most of their games on Astroturf, it is the shoe they wear most frequently.

The studded shoe with six nylon studs is used for muddy fields and soft ground. The studs penetrate into the ground to give the player proper traction; they come in different lengths and widths for different field conditions.

Many coaches and players are not aware of the importance of shoe selection. Whenever we are playing on a grass field, the players and I go to the field about an hour before game time to inspect it. I

Molded-rubber shoe used on Astroturf. This is the most widely used of all soccer shoes in the United States.

The studded shoe is used on muddy fields and other soft grounds. A metal wrench called a key is used to screw studs onto the shoe.

press my index finger down into the turf; if my finger sinks into the ground, my decision will be studs. On several occasions, it has begun to rain during the first half of a game. The moment we got to the locker room at half time the players changed their molded-rubber shoes for studded ones. In another game, the field was frozen solid when the game began, but, during the first half, the sun came out and the field's surface began to thaw. We started the game in molded-rubber shoes, and the players were slipping and falling all over the slick surface. At half time, the players changed to studs. Our opponents did not change and at one point in the second half our forward scored an easy goal when their defender fell while trying to change direction on the slick surface.

Soccer shoes should fit like gloves, which means they must be broken in properly. A common way of breaking in a shoe is to lace the shoe on your foot and soak it in a tub of warm water for a few minutes so that the leather will soften and conform to the shape of your foot. Then, you walk in them for 20 to 30 minutes while they are still wet. (This is a good time to mow your lawn.)

In addition to being broken in carefully, soccer shoes should be polished regularly to keep the leather soft and pliable and to keep them looking good. A dull, unpolished shoe is a dead giveaway that a player is a rookie.

6

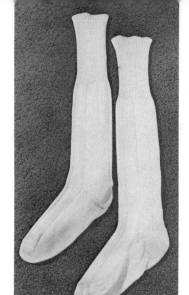

Soccer hose

Shin pads, inserted between stocking and shin to protect against injuries.

Stockings

The best type of stockings are soccer hose, which have a foot in them like regular socks. They should be pulled up over the calf muscle and tied just below the break in the knee. The tie-on, a gauze strip which is used to hold the sock in place, should not be tied so tightly that it impedes circulation but tightly enough to hold the stocking in place.

Shin Pads

Shin pads are placed under the stockings to protect the shins from any kicks, which could cause serious cuts, bruises, or even fractures. The shin pad should not be very thick or it will hinder your control. If you do not have shin pads, you always can make a pair from a lightweight magazine such as *Sports Illustrated*.

THE BALL

Soccer balls come in many different varieties, but all official balls have a 27-inch diameter and are made of leather. In the "early

7

Soccer balls. Size 5 (left) is used by teens and professionals; size 4 (right) is designed for younger players.

days," balls were made with 8 panels. Later, they were made with 16 panels, and, today, the number of panels has been increased to 32. The reason is that the larger leather panels in 8- and 16- panel balls stretched after use, causing the ball to increase in size. Someone realized that if the panels were smaller, there would be less stretching. However, with the modern methods of water-proofing and synthetics, panels stretch very little today. Therefore, we will probably go back to 16- or 8-panel balls again; they require less stitching, which is the most difficult and time-consuming process in ball manufacturing.

The most popular ball in the United States is the 32-panel black-and-white. The black and white panels give the player an idea of the spin on the ball. This ball has given soccer an identity in the United States, and, personally, I think it is the best type of ball. Many black-and-white panel balls lose their shape quickly because of inferior stitching. If you intend to purchase a new ball, pick out a reputable company and buy their top-line ball. This will assure you of proper stitching and weight.

Wet weather, also, affects soccer balls. A ball that is not water-proof tends to get heavy when it is wet and then to get hard as the leather dries. Cheaper balls lose their shape. Today, most top-flight leather balls are being plastic-coated, which makes them practically waterproof.

If you own a ball, purchase special leather- or ball-cleaner and clean your ball regularly, particularly if it gets wet or muddy. (Let it dry before you clean it.) Also, deflating the ball after use will prolong its life, since the air pressure exerts a stretching effect on the panels and stitches. If the ball is not waterproof or if the water-proofing wears off, you can protect the ball with special water-proofing sprays or silicone.

If you are below 12 years of age, buy a number 4 ball. (All regulation balls are number 5.) This is slightly smaller in diameter and lighter in weight. It is important that when you kick a ball you get a good result, and if the ball is too heavy, you may get discouraged.

GOALKEEPING EQUIPMENT

Since the goalkeeper has special responsibilities, he frequently needs special equipment. For instance, on days when the sun is increasing the glare or shining into the goalkeeper's eyes, he must wear a hat. Any baseball or golf hat with a brim that reduces glare is fine. This hat must be part of the goalkeeper's game equipment, and he should practice using a hat every chance he gets.

The most important part of the goalkeeper's equipment, however, is his gloves. Goalkeeper gloves, generally, are made out of cotton or wool (insuring washability), and have rubber strips with small rubber nubs to help prevent slipping. However, simple cotton garden gloves also work well.

When a leather ball gets wet or muddy, it is as difficult to catch as a greased pig. When a wet ball coming at the goalkeeper at approximately 70 to 100 miles per hour must be caught or deflected,

Goalkeeper shirt and gloves. The goalkeeper wears a solid-color shirt of a different color from the other players' shirts, and gloves for better control of the ball.

gloves help tremendously. The goalkeeper's hands become wet and slippery when it rains, too, and gloves are a solution to this problem, as well.

This past season, when the Atoms played Dallas in Texas Stadium, it began to rain hard, just before kickoff. Our goalkeeper, Bob Rigby, elected not to use his gloves. Early in the first half, a Dallas player hit a spinning cross (ball hit from near the sideline across the field) meant for their outstanding striker, Kyle Rote. The ball was misdirected right to Bob Rigby. Bob placed his hands behind the ball for a routine save and started looking for an Atom to throw it to. He didn't need one; the ball slipped through his hands and ended up in the back of the net for the winning Dallas goal. Bob's loss of concentration (looking to throw before the ball had been caught) was a blunder. But, in my mind, his biggest error was not wearing his gloves. I am positive that goal would not have been made if Bob had been using his gloves.

In extremely cold weather, too, goalkeeper's gloves are almost a must. If goalkeepers don't wear gloves and their fingers get like stones from the cold, they can't possibly catch a cross or shot. At first, all goalkeepers complain that gloves are bulky and cause them to lose their feel for the ball. But, with several practice sessions, they learn that gloves can be worn without loss of skill. If you are a future professional goalkeeper and want to perform at top form, you must add a pair of gloves to your equipment bag. They play a vital role in safe goalkeeping in wet weather (rain or mud), when the grass gets wet (night games), and in extremely cold weather.

Soccer is an inexpensive sport. But, as I said at the chapter's beginning, don't purchase cheap equipment. Particularly, your shoes must fit well and be of high-quality leather, since your feet are your most important consideration.

chapter two

No matter what a soccer player's age or ability, he will not be of great value to his team if he is not superbly physically fit. A player must be able to run fast, turn quickly, bend and dodge, kick and volley with the same determination in the last minute of the game as in the first minute. And this degree of fitness throughout a team is a major step towards winning a championship.

SPECIFIC SOCCER FITNESS

Fitness for soccer is much more comprehensive and demanding than fitness for most other sports. An endurance runner or swimmer would find his fitness inadequate for soccer. A tremendously fit boxer would probably not be able to last a full soccer

how to get in shape

game. To play soccer to the best of his ability, a soccer player must be in top shape in respect to five different aspects of physical fitness: endurance, speed, agility, flexibility, and strength. *Specific soccer fitness must be one goal of all soccer players.*

ENDURANCE

The game of soccer is in fact an endurance game. There are no timeouts and very few substitutions. Games are 90 minutes long with only one 10-minute break at half time. Therefore, endurance becomes a factor of major importance. There are two types of endurance taken into consideration when training the soccer player—cardiovascular and muscular.

Cardiovascular Endurance

Cardiovascular endurance, in simple terms, is the ability of the cardiovascular system to support the body's increased activity over an extended time period. In order for muscles to function properly during exercise, they need a considerable amount of oxygen above and beyond the normal amount. Proper training prepares the cardiovascular system to meet the muscles' increased oxygen demands efficiently by increasing the amount of oxygen intake with each heartbeat. Basically, the trained heart pumps additional blood through the lungs, so more oxygen is picked up and distributed to the muscles. With correct training methods, this type of endurance can be increased anywhere from 40 to 70 percent.

There is an old myth that running laps or long distances is the best method to increase cardiovascular endurance, but experts have found that there is a far better method of training that achieves maximum results in a shorter amount of time—working out in intervals. (When I was a player, I always felt running laps was a boring chore and that that would be justification enough for their elimination.)

If you think about it, soccer itself is played in intervals. You make a run with the ball, have a shot on goal, and then someone else takes over and you have a rest period. So the best possible training method for soccer players is hard physical training soccer-style. The game requires maximum effort in sprinting, changing directions, jumping, and other heavy, physical exercise; so you should run sprints with changes of direction—with and without the ball—for 15 or 30 seconds with a rest interval of the same time between each run. Sometimes in a game your rest period is longer, and sometimes you are required to make a run forward and immediately chase an opponent to try to win the ball back. Therefore, on occasion you should double your rest interval, as well as your work period.

In the Atoms' practices I work on the interval system of work and rest for a total period of 90 minutes with only a 10-minute break after 45 minutes, which is called half time, the same as in a regular game. I would suggest that you build your practice time up

The final results of hard training are victory and the ecstasy it brings.
Atoms' George O'Neill (11) tops the celebration.

gradually—working 30 minutes the first week and slowly increasing to 70 or 90 minutes. Keep in mind that the interval system requires your working hard for 15 to 30 seconds and then resting for the same amount of time.

But during the rest interval, don't rest completely. Rather, do flexibility exercises and ball juggling (keeping the ball in the air by bouncing it off the head, chest, thighs, or feet). In this way you improve your ball skills while resting.

Also, any running done in training should be interspersed with running that requires dribbling the ball. This is true for several reasons. The ball is magic in that all of us enjoy manipulating it in many different ways; I find that all players work exceptionally hard with a ball at their feet and rarely, if ever, have the feeling of boredom. Also, when a ball is at your feet, you run differently, with shorter steps. Since much of the running in a game is done with a ball, lots of practice is absolutely essential.

I am sure that you will get great results from this type of training and will find the game easy even in the last minute.

Muscular Endurance

The second type of endurance is muscle endurance. Your leg muscles undergo heavy strain during a game; they must be trained so that they will be flexible (stretching exercises) and strong (leg strengthening exercises) even in a game's last moments. Leg muscles must be able to absorb the strain of jumping, kicking, tackling, and running. Proper strengthening exercises along with soccer playing and practice develop the leg muscles to this necessary level of competence.

Enduring arm strength is also necessary to keep the arms from feeling heavy after long periods of running.

And abdominal strength is vitally important in total body strength. First of all, this muscle sheath protects many of your vital organs from heavy blows by the ball and opponents' knees and elbows. Secondly, abdominal development eliminates extra weight, which settles there in the unconditioned athlete. (Any extra weight will hinder endurance and movement.) And many abdominal exercises strengthen the back, too. Since a soccer player twists and turns and receives many bumps while in awkward positions, back injuries can occur; only strength enables a player to avoid them. I have always believed that, if the middle of the man is strong, the rest will come easily.

Almost every soccer exercise listed in this chapter is designed to develop muscle endurance and cardiovascular endurance at the same time. Even when you are juggling the ball, which is a relatively easy and restful exercise, you still are helping train yourself and it still relates to both types of endurance.

SPEED

There are two ways a player can be fast. The first is the obvious—speed while running. When I look for players, I look for

Philadelphia's George O'Neill (11) uses his explosive speed to burst past New York Cosmos defender Malcolm Dawes (20). Deiter Zajdel (22) and Ralph Wright (14) of New York rush O'Neill in defense of their goalkeeper, Jerry Sularz.

17

Speed through efficient ball control is the key to Atom Karl Minor's (in white) success here where he is dribbling out of a crowd—pushing the ball into open space and sprinting away from opponents.

explosive running speed—from a start over a distance of 10 or 15 yards. This type of speed is essential, and most great players have it. Running speed, however, is the one aspect of the game which does not improve much through training (5 through 10 percent). Running speed is primarily a God-given talent.

On the other hand, there is a type of speed that can be improved enormously—speed through efficient ball control. The player who has total confidence in his ball control skills will work more efficiently and be a much faster player. And there is no limit to development in this direction.

Obviously, the best players combine explosive speed with excellent ball control. For instance, Warren Archibald of the Miami Toros, the 1973 North American Soccer League's Most Valuable Player, has tremendous explosive speed over the first 20 yards and top-flight dribbling, passing, and shooting techniques. It is because he combines these qualities that he is a dangerous soccer player.

AGILITY

Stiff, straight-ahead players are lost in soccer. Soccer players must have agility—the ability to change direction quickly. This is especially necessary for forwards. Andy Provan, called "The Flea," who has been our leading scorer for the past two seasons, sometimes changes direction 20 or 30 times while dribbling. When he sees his defender's weight shifting, he quickly changes direction and goes by. When I first saw him play in England, I sat near the top of the stadium; from there his quick changes of direction reminded me of a flea's movements; the name stuck.

We all have a fair amount of agility. When I watch boys and girls play tag, I see fantastic agility. Just when it appears they are going to be tagged, they change direction and speed. This is exactly what must be developed with a ball at your feet.

Almost all types of practice with the ball and against an opponent are directly related to agility training. As a matter of fact, we play dribble tag at center circle. Another good way to develop agility is in one-on-one practice situations. For instance, in our Atoms' practice, if Andy Provan dribbles by Bob Smith, Bobby will be forced to change direction quickly and chase Andy in an attempt to prevent a goal. In this situation, both players are improving their agility—Bob without the ball and Andy with the ball. One versus one, with two goals approximately 30 yards apart, is one of the best practices I know for players from six to professional age.

Agility can be improved. Our first-round draft choice this year, rookie Tom Galati, lacked the agility to become a great player. Specific agility practices have helped him tremendously. Con-

19

Atoms' Jim Fryatt demonstrates the power of agility, nudging the ball forward to avoid a tackle and quickly stepping over the slashing feet of a Washington defender.

fidence with the ball, knowledge of when to change direction quickly, and practice always pay dividends.

FLEXIBILITY

Flexibility is necessary to avoid injury. A muscle is like a garden hose. If the hose is out in the hot sun, you can twist it any direction with no problem; but if that same hose gets cold it becomes stiff and uncooperative and will break at the slightest twist or pull. In soccer, your body is going to be placed in many unnatural positions. It must be supple, so when this happens the muscles cooperate without chance of injury. There is quite a bit of physical contact in soccer, and a player avoids many injuries if he has good flexibility.

A minor muscle pull (strain) or tear can keep a player out for weeks. George O'Neill, our outstanding midfield player, who has a heart like a lion's, had an outstanding season in 1973. But, because of a minor muscle pull, he never found the same form in 1974. He played every game with this injury, but that half step he lost hurt him more than the pain he experienced.

All types of stretching exercises are important in a player's daily training, and they should be an integral part of his warm-up, too. Flexibility exercises are vital when warming up. It is necessary to stretch the large muscles and get the blood circulating through them. A warmed-up muscle rarely gets injured unless a blow is landed on it directly, and, even then, the injury will be far less acute.

STRENGTH

Players must also be strong. However, the giant muscle man probably would not be a good soccer player. Specific strengths are necessary, mainly for jumping (legs), striking a ball (legs), power in the tackle (legs), and muscle endurance needed for long-distance running (legs, abdomen, and arms).

None of my players carry on an extensive training program with weights, though we do use weight training for rehabilitation after injuries. Proper weight training can be helpful in gaining additional muscle strength, but it never will be a substitute for specific soccer training. Also, I am wary of weight training, particularly for the young player, because any overdevelopment of a muscle group can affect the soccer player in a negative way. Therefore, I do not ad-

21

vocate weight training. Rather, use daily shooting practice to develop leg strength and to help shooting technique. And do other exercises, such as those at the end of this chapter, to develop other strengths.

DAILY PROGRAM

General Health Rules

There is another vital aspect of fitness: A player must take care of himself. Getting proper rest, eating the proper food, and exercising the proper mental discipline to avoid harmful habits such as drugs or alcohol are as important as training for fitness.

Athletes are judged on the field, but their off-the-field activities play an important part in their performances. Only you can control your life-style. This self-discipline has many positive carry-overs. Your ability to say no at any time makes you tougher than you can possibly imagine.

I cannot emphasize enough the importance of creating for yourself an attitude of total commitment. I have seen a lot of great talents never make it because of their inability to discipline themselves. My advice to young players is always the same. Put everything you have into the game, and the rewards and experience will far exceed all the sacrifices.

Regular Exercise

On the following pages, a variety of exercises (with and without the ball) that I use with my players are diagrammed. Most of these exercises overlap; so, while you are doing an exercise for speed, you are increasing leg strength, endurance, etc., too. I suggest you select three or four exercises from each group for use in a daily program.

However, the very best kind of fitness training of all is to play. Soccer is a conditioning sport. No one except the goalkeeper stands around; the breaks are short and everybody gets involved. By practicing or playing daily, the proper muscle groups will become soccer fit.

22

SPEED

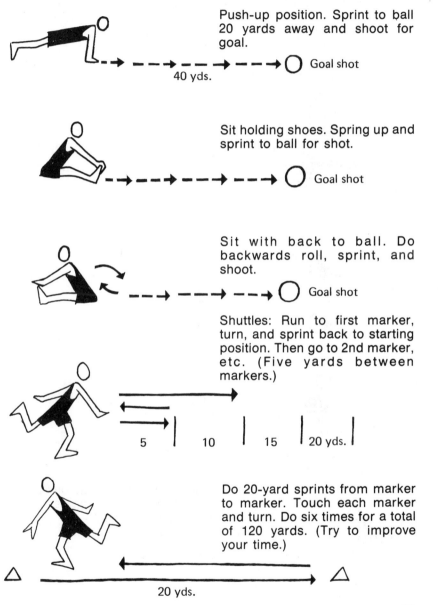

Push-up position. Sprint to ball 20 yards away and shoot for goal.

40 yds.

Goal shot

Sit holding shoes. Spring up and sprint to ball for shot.

Goal shot

Sit with back to ball. Do backwards roll, sprint, and shoot.

Goal shot

Shuttles: Run to first marker, turn, and sprint back to starting position. Then go to 2nd marker, etc. (Five yards between markers.)

5 10 15 20 yds.

Do 20-yard sprints from marker to marker. Touch each marker and turn. Do six times for a total of 120 yards. (Try to improve your time.)

20 yds.

23

AGILITY

 Dribble slalom-style through markers 3 to 5 yards apart.

 With partner on hands and knees, jump from side to side over partner's back.

 Jump side to side *over* the ball.

 Jump forward and back *over* the ball.

 While dribbling, change direction quickly and run fast with ball for 5 to 10 yards. (Repeat.)

FLEXIBILITY

Arching up from a prone position, lift knees and arms off ground and hold for 5 seconds.

Sit facing each other, join hands, and pull forward and backward, keeping legs straight.

One player sits; the other stands and pushes forward on back.

Sitting back to back, exchange ball by twisting in opposite direction. Then turn and pass the other way.

Stand back to back; pass ball between legs; then pass over head. Alternate.

FLEXIBILITY

 Lie on back. Roll ball under back and around waist to other side—return to lying position and repeat.

 While sitting, roll ball around feet and back.

 Stand with legs apart. Roll ball in figure 8 around feet.

 Take prone position. Arch up and bounce ball with hands. Alternate bounce.

 Stand with legs apart. Hold ball between legs with one hand behind legs and one hand in front. Then change hands from front to back and catch the ball in same motion.

26

STRENGTH

Do push-ups on top of ball—10 to 30.

Run, jump, hang in air, and slam ball to ground, with right hand, then left hand, then two hands.

Take push-up position, head to head, and attempt to pull opponent off balance.

In push-up position, head ball back to thrower.

In crab position, head ball back to thrower.

27

LEGS

Jump and bring knees to chest. Repeat 10 to 30 times.

Jump, bring heels up in back, and arch back in heading position. Repeat 10 to 30 times.

Jump and spread legs apart. Repeat 10 to 30 times.

Jump and touch toes with legs held straight. Repeat 10 to 30 times.

Pinch ball between heels, jump and throw ball up over head, and catch. Repeat 10 to 30 times.

LEGS

Jump, hang in air, throw ball from behind, and head to partner.

Partner stands and holds ball above head. Jump and head ball—land, jump, land, jump. Repeat 10 to 30 times.

Run parallel to partner, take off on one leg, jump, hang, and head ball back to partner. Run to opposite side (jump off foot nearest to partner and repeat, etc).

Lie on back, throw ball up, get up and control ball, and begin juggling before the ball lands on ground.

ABDOMINALS

Sit on partner's knees. He holds your feet. Bend backward to limit and return to upright sitting position. Repeat 10 to 30 times.

Partner holds feet at waist level. Sit up and touch your toes. Repeat 10 to 30 times.

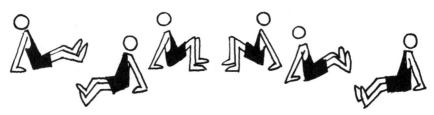

Sit opposite partner with legs parallel. Change position by withdrawing legs and extending legs to opposite side. Repeat 10 to 30 times.

Stand and hold the legs of partner who is on ground facing away. Push legs toward ground (hard thrust). Player on ground allows legs to go but stops feet just before hitting ground, then raises legs again, keeping them straight. Repeat 10 to 30 times.

V-sit and move alternate legs up and down. Pass ball between legs with each exchange. Figure eight ball around legs.

ABDOMINALS

Pinch ball between feet. Roll backward and take ball in hands. Bring ball back to original position. Repeat 10 to 30 times.

Lie on back with ball in hands overhead. V-sit and touch ball to shoes and back. Repeat 10 to 30 times.

V-sit with ball between feet. Bring knee up to chest and return to straight position.

V-sit, legs extended to side six inches off the ground with arms extended in opposite direction of legs. Change quickly back and forth.

V-sit and roll ball around and under raised legs.

chapter three

A player cannot begin to enjoy the game of soccer properly until he achieves a certain level of mastery and feeling for rhythm with the ball. This is very difficult, because the ball is controlled much of the time by the feet. Using one's feet is unnatural; almost every ordinary activity utilizes the hands. We comb our hair, brush our teeth, write and feed ourselves, all with our hands. All these skills were developed through constant repetition. The same principle must be applied to developing soccer techniques.

For years in America, we have been playing soccer. However, because of lack of exposure, many rule makers, coaches, and referees have never seen a game in its highest form. As a result, they develop coaching techniques that produce short-term rather than long-term success.

techniques

In my opinion, a player enjoys two aspects of the game most: scoring goals and having possession of the ball. Both of these aspects require skills—basic techniques—that should be taught.

The most important aspects of training for young players are development of a love for their sport and a foundation to go onward and upward. This requires a great deal of emphasis on *technique*. After several years in the game, the young player should have developed the basic fundamentals of passing, ball control, dribbling, heading, and kicking. It is my experience that many players in high school and college still lack these basic abilities. The old game of kick-it-up-the-field-and-chase-it is still prevalent. But reckless kicking produces little and takes much of the enjoyment out of the game for the players.

When a team masters the ability to put 10 or 15 passes together, it generally wins.

LEARNING TECHNIQUES

It is my feeling that we are far behind in technique development in America. Youth coaches need to put much more emphasis on perfecting the necessary fundamental skills. When players are satisfied with faulty techniques, they are hindered when the competition level is advanced. One of the biggest problems is coaches who lack the ability to demonstrate. If a coach shows a player how to pass but passes awkwardly himself, the player will get a bad mental picture of the technique. It is difficult to correct him later.

It is also important to avoid too much emphasis on one technique. Soccer is similar to basketball in that both games require mastery of all the skills involved; specialization in just one or two of them is not enough. For instance, many youngsters who desire to become good basketball players make the mistake of practicing only their shooting while failing to work on dribbling, passing, rebounding, and defense.

The same can be said of soccer. Oftentimes, young players overemphasize one technique; in most cases, the skill involved is ball control. Players quickly learn that a fun way to help improve their ball control (but certainly not the way to master complete control) is by juggling the ball with the various parts of the body. This entails keeping the ball up in the air by using the feet, thighs, chest and head. Although this type of technique training may help you to a limited extent, it should not be overemphasized at the expense of mastering the others.

Those players that fail to develop all the techniques and merely spend their time on one or two aspects of the game never become the complete team man all players need to be. The good player spends roughly the same amount of time working on all parts of his game with any extra training devoted to those aspects in which he is weakest. He strives to become skilled not only in ball control, but in dribbling, passing, heading, shooting, and kicking, too.

34

Lew Meehl of Philadelphia demonstrates fine kicking form. His high follow-through gives him maximum power and lifts the ball high over his opponents.

Simple play is very effective. Fancy stuff is not needed to be a good player. My best players with the Atoms are the ones who have the simple techniques mastered completely. If a player plays a simple ball to one of his teammates and runs into a position to receive the ball, he has done a great job. Or when a player keeps possession of the ball until the right moment comes to make a "killer" pass, again he has enjoyed success.

PACING

Another problem that I see frequently is players who are running at top speed most of the game. Obviously, a skill becomes very difficult to execute when a player is running too fast. Slow down so that you can control the ball and yourself. Save your speed and your energy for times when you need it. On most occasions, the slow approach will be not only the safest but also the quickest way to success. If you have ever watched Pele play, you know he wanders around at a very slow pace during much of the game. He kind of lulls defenders into his rhythm; then he produces the unexpected with a burst of speed away from them and into a good position to score. He saves his speed for the time when it counts.

IMPROVING TECHNIQUES

Once young players have a correct idea of what a particular technique involves, experience tells me they can improve their ability, themselves, by constant practice with the ball. Just simply passing or striking a ball against a wall is an excellent practice, since it involves accuracy, speed of pass, and learning to control the ball as it rebounds from the wall. The more you play and practice with the ball, the more you develop the feel and coordination in your feet that you have developed in your hands. With the passing of time and practice, you will be amazed at the great amount of skill and control that you will be able to acquire.

Imitating the pros can be very healthy at this stage, because the pros use simple techniques to perfection. The advanced player has refined his techniques and can utilize them skillfully in game situations.

In the following chapters, I discuss the techniques that soccer players need in a game. All players must learn to use these techniques except the goalkeeper, whose unique and challenging position requires yet another set of skills.

The game of soccer becomes simple once the basic techniques are mastered. Mastery of skill increases confidence and efficiency. It increases the speed of the game. I once heard an expression that is a good motto for any soccer player who is practicing technique: "Make it simple, make it quick."

SAMPLE PROGRAM

It is important to make up a program for yourself to help you develop technique. The following is a sample program.

Allow one minute for each of the following exercises:
1. Head juggling
2. Dribbling—practice tight ball control
3. Thigh juggling
4. Dribbling—practice changing direction quickly
5. Instep juggling
6. Dribbling—practice changing speeds—start slowly and accelerate for a distance of 10 yards, and then go slowly again.
7. Combined juggling—combine head, thigh, and instep juggling.
8. Dribbling—combine change of direction and speed.

After doing each of the exercises for one minute, start over and repeat each exercise for one minute more.

Spend 10 minutes working on ball control. Throw or kick ball against a wall. Control ball on return and repeat. If you have a partner, have him throw or kick ball to you.

Work for 15 minutes on all types of passing. Set up targets at 10-yard, 20-yard, and 30-yard distances. (Chairs, shirts, rocks, etc., can be used as targets.) Start passing stationary balls and then dribble to spot and pass while moving. Use both your right and left feet to pass.

Work for 10 minutes each on dribbling and heading. To practice dribbling, set up an obstacle course using trees, shirts, chairs, sticks, rocks, etc., and dribble around it to the finish line; strive for top speed and ball control while dribbling. To practice heading, head the ball against a wall, striving to keep it in motion; count the number of repititions and try to improve every day. Stand close to wall while heading.

This entire program should take you about an hour and 15 minutes to complete. A daily program like this will improve your techniques tremendously. I have found that constant repetition is the key to technique practice.

chapter four

One of the most important techniques to develop is the ability to control all types of balls that come to you in a game. You must be able to select the methods of control, take the pace off the ball by catching it, and then perform the next technique the game situation requires, i.e. pass, shoot, clear, or dribble. You will receive many types of balls in a game, and this is what makes ball control complex. No matter at what height the ball comes to you, an instant decision must be made as to how to pluck it out of the air so that the ball doesn't rebound away from you.

If I were to kick a hard shot against a mattress hanging from the goal (crossbar), the ball would hit and fall to the ground almost directly below where it hit, with the mattress absorbing all the speed of the ball. But the same shot hit against the side of your house

ball control

would bounce far away, out of control. Your object in controlling the ball is to get it to drop in front of you as if it had hit a mattress. To do this you "cushion" the ball, give with it to soften its impact. You can cushion a ball with your head, chest, thigh, instep, or the inside of your foot. By relaxing and "giving" at the time of the ball's impact, you will deaden the ball's momentum and it will drop to the ground right in front of you, in perfect position to be moved closer to your opponent's goal by whatever method you select.

I have taught young, inexperienced players to catch balls without giving them any advice other than what part of the body to use. It always amazes me how quickly they work out all of the problems for themselves; soon they are catching my thrown balls like pros. This simply means that repetition develops skill.

FOUR BASIC STEPS

The following four steps should always be practiced when controlling a ball:
1. Look around (know what is around you);
2. Catch the ball (cushioning effect);
3. Control the ball on the ground (don't allow falling ball to bounce); and
4. Select the next technique the game requires (pass, dribble, shoot).

Ball control out of the air requires a certain rhythm (sense of timing) between player and ball. This rhythm can be greatly improved by ball juggling using the parts of the body required for ball control.

CATCHES

Head Catch

Many balls come to you at head height. Position yourself so that you are behind the ball, keep your eyes on the ball, and watch it as it hits your forehead (at the hairline). Just as the ball is about to hit your head, withdraw your head ever so slightly. By giving with the ball, you achieve the cushioning effect. Your forehead should be slightly tilted upward so that the ball pops up. Allow the ball to drop to the ground and trap it with one part of your foot (more will be said about trapping the ball later in the chapter).

Practice throwing balls in the air and catching them with your forehead. If you can take high balls and catch them and begin head juggling, you are ready to try kicked balls from various distances. You will find this ball-control technique quite easy after some practice.

Chest Catch

Balls received below head level but well above the ground should be caught with the chest. The chest catch is much more efficient than

Skip Roderick of the Atoms shows the form necessary to make a successful chest catch.

Kit Fagan demonstrates the thigh catch—eyes on ball, leg relaxed, good balance.

the head catch and is the easiest of all catches, since you have such a large surface with which to catch the ball.

Again, you must get fully behind the ball. Arch your back to tilt your chest up. As the ball hits your chest, relax by moving your shoulders in a forward motion. Done correctly, the ball nearly sticks to your chest and pops up just a little. When the ball falls to the ground, again, you use one of the methods of control listed under trapping.

Thigh Catch

Certain high balls can be taken on top of your thigh. The secret is to bring your knee up so that your thigh is like a landing pad. Relax your leg and let the ball hit between your knee and hip; the thigh cushions the falling ball. Many beginners make the error of pulling their leg away (downward) as the ball hits. This is wrong, because the ball will fall too far in front of you to control. Keep your leg fixed in a 90° angle and relax. Again, as the ball falls to the ground, use one of the traps explained later.

Instep Catch

Good players actually can catch balls on their instep. Bobby Smith and Tom Galati, two backs with the Atoms, use the instep catch to control many of the low goalkeeper's throws they receive during a game. Being able to control the ball almost instantly with their instep gives these players time to evaluate the situation around them, so they can make the correct decision on what next should be done with the ball.

The instep catch requires tremendous timing and feel for the ball. Although you won't be able to catch the ball and have it stay on your instep, you will find the ball falling very close to your feet. Again, the secret is relaxation. Watch the ball all the way to your foot. Place your foot slightly forward and just off the ground, positioning it so the ball hits near the toe area. (The ball should land on top of the toes, not on the end of your toe.) Don't lift your foot up too far or you will lose your balance. As the ball hits your foot, let your foot hang limp.

Karl Minor demonstrates the instep catch.

Practice by throwing the ball up and catching it. After several tosses, you will find the ball staying close to you where you easily can dribble, pass or shoot.

Inside-of-foot Catch

The inside-of-foot catch is often used on low, hard-driven passes. The inside of the foot has a broad surface, so the ball is less likely to slip off the foot than when the instep catch is used. Also, the inside-of-foot catch drops the ball directly in front of you where you can pass, shoot, start dribbling, or clear.

Balance is a big factor in this catch, as it is in almost all soccer skills, and only practice will provide you with the necessary posture for good control. You can practice by hitting balls against a wall and using the inside-of-foot catch to stop return balls. Or practice with a friend as the Atoms do. Frequently, Atoms players warm up by standing approximately 10 yards apart and hitting fairly hard drives at each other's feet. Invariably they use the inside-of-foot catch to take the pace off the ball. Practice will enable you to angle your foot correctly so that the ball ends up in front of you rather than popping up in the air.

Outside-of-foot Catch

Sometimes, in a game, you receive bouncing balls or hard-driven passes while you are sideways to the ball. If time does not allow you to turn and face the ball, you can catch it by using the outside of your foot. Basically, the catch is the same as the instep catch, except the ball is caught to the side rather than in front of you. The outside of your foot, also, is very effective to control rolling balls from a side direction.

TRAPS

The next step is to combine the catch with a trap. To play the ball you have caught effectively, you must bring it under control the instant it hits the ground by trapping it with some part of your foot so it can't bounce away. Your foot becomes a wedge over the ball. Trapping a ball is simply quieting the ball down. Once the ball falls to the ground, it must not be allowed to bounce again. Stay on your toes when catching the ball, so that you can quickly get in position for the trap.

Sole-of-foot Trap

To trap the ball with the sole of your foot, poise your foot slightly

The inside-of-foot catch, executed here by Lew Meehl (above), and the outside-of-foot catch, by Stan Startzell (facing page), are executed basically in the same way but with opposite sides of the foot.

47

above the ball just as it lands on the ground. As the ball bounces up, it will be stopped by the sole of your foot. It will be at a full stop and totally under control.

Don't step on the ball! Allow just enough space for the ball to bounce up to the foot.

This trap can be used after head, chest, thigh, instep, and outside-of-foot catches and should be used whenever you want to go forward.

Inside-of-foot Trap

The inside-of-foot trap is used to move the ball sideways; it is probably the most commonly used trap, as the sideways movement is very natural. Just as in the sole-of-foot trap, place the inside of your foot directly over and slightly above the ball just as it lands on the ground. Lean in the direction you want to go.

Outside-of-foot Trap

In the outside-of-foot trap, also used to move the ball sideways, the player places the outside of his foot over the ball just as it lands on the ground. Again, you must lean in the direction you want to move. Your trapping foot is placed across in front of your stationary foot, and the ball is dragged sideways by the trapping foot.

PRACTICE

Only constant practice will enable you to attain perfect ball control. Have your friends throw or kick balls at you and practice catching them, keeping score on good and bad. I can stand just a short distance from my players and kick hard balls at them. They catch these balls naturally and enjoy the practice.

The higher you go in soccer, the more important perfect ball control becomes. You must learn to catch or stop every ball that comes

Jim Fryatt of Philadelphia is bringing the ball down to the ground and dribbling it at the same time. By putting the ball on the ground, Jim realizes he will have far better control of the ball and therefore will be a more dangerous player.

to you in a game. The fact that you cannot use your hands makes soccer unique and your task more difficult. As your ability to catch and trap improves, you will find yourself missing your hands less and less. When this happens, you are well on your way to becoming a soccer player.

chapter five

Dribbling is another necessary skill, and top players like Pele of Brazil and Johann Cruyff of Holland are masters of this art. Many times in a game a player finds all of his teammates tightly marked. Then he has to dribble. Skillful dribblers create goals with their talent, and every coach looks for outstanding dribblers to add to his team.

The ability to dribble by an opponent, especially if you are out on a wing (standing relatively close to one of the sidelines) where there will probably be only one defender, will frequently allow you to generate a dangerous attack. Steve David and Warren Archibald, both of the Miami Toros, are two of the best strikers (central forwards) in the North American Soccer League when it comes to dribbling by opposition defenders. Every time either one of them

dribbling

takes off with the ball, they are a threat to their opponent's goal. They may score themselves or set up a goal for another player.

Many players have learned to play soccer in their backyards, which surprisingly is a very natural way to develop dribbling. Usually, in these games, one boy plays against a friend with makeshift goals; since they have no one to pass to, dribbling becomes essential. This practice is necessary to a player's development.

Pros also practice this way. It is not unusual, before the Atoms formal practice starts, to find a pair of players like Barry Barto and Tom Galati playing a minigame between themselves. They practice their mastered feints (deceptive moves), along with some new ones, while trying to dribble by each other. Dribbling in a minigame forces you to get in the proper habit of keeping your head up and your eyes on your opponent most of the time.

DRIBBLING SKILLS

Basically, good dribbling involves the following skills:
1. Close control of the ball
2. Ability to change speed
3. Ability to change direction
4. Ability to feint (fake)
5. Ability to keep eyes up to see what is happening around you (peripheral vision)

You can set up an obstacle course which will require change of direction dribbling. Also practice going forward and changing direction (either sideways or turn and go back) quickly.

Barry Barto exhibits dribbling skill as he leans in a balanced way to change the direction of the ball.

Feinting (or Faking)

Some players are naturally good at feinting, the art of deceiving an opponent through movement; others require much practice but do develop feinting ability. Mike Renshaw, of the Dallas Tornado, feints as well as anyone in the NASL. Plenty of opponents attempting to steal the ball from him end up on the seat of their pants in Dallas Stadium, and his superlative feints are usually what puts them there. Mike obviously was born with some of the ability he has at feinting, but you can be sure he has spent years working to improve it.

Many tricks with and without the ball are used by good dribblers to confuse their opponents. One of these is head and shoulder feinting—dropping your head or shoulders to the left and then going right. Stepping to one side makes opponents think you are going that direction, but the moment they begin to move in that direction, you go the other way quickly.

An elementary feint done well is much better than a complicated feint that you cannot do efficiently. The great Pele even deceives defenders with eye feints.

I am certain that the one-against-one game in the backyard will bring out some of your feints. Then constant practice will improve both your technique and your confidence until soon you will begin using naturally the feints that are successful for you.

Close Control

As with many other soccer skills, development of good dribbling involves mastering the feet. One important secret is to nudge rather than kick the ball. You can use the inside of your foot, the outside of your foot, or your instep to manipulate it. Obviously, your running style is different with a ball at your feet, and short choppy steps are a trademark of all outstanding dribblers.

The ball should be touched on practically every other step, and a good practice is to dribble touching the ball with each step. This will develop your sense of balance and timing with the ball at your feet.

Balance and close control of the ball are very important, particularly if the opponent gives a strong challenge. Here, Allan Spavin of Washington protects the ball even though Barry Barto (Atoms) tries to take it away.

Change of Speed

To be a good dribbler, you must be able to control the ball at different speeds. For instance, you should approach an opponent at half speed and then when you decide to go past him accelerate to

54

Dribbling by an opponent requires a quick burst of speed so that you can get your body between the opponent and the ball. Here Juan Paletta (in white) of Philadelphia has made his move by Coyne of Boston.

top speed—blast off like a rocket. Then you will have several advantages on your opponent. First, he does not know when you are going to start sprinting. Secondly, he has his back to where you are facing. Thirdly, if you use a feint to get him off balance, a burst of speed will give you a better chance to get away with it.

Atoms' Andy Provan uses outside-of-foot catch to change directions and get away from N.Y. Cosmos' Len Renery.

Change in Direction

You must also practice changing direction. If you only go forward, your opponent will have an easy job stealing the ball away from you. Learn to use one foot to turn the ball while you pivot on the other foot in the direction you want to go. You can change the direction of the ball with the inside or outside of your foot, though the outside of the foot is most commonly used.

56

Using Your Eyes

When you first begin playing soccer, the job of controlling the ball at your feet is difficult enough, and your eyes are glued to the ground. But, as you become more familiar with the ball, you will be able to look around while controlling it, until, you will be able to see

New York's Barry Mahy wisely looks up, while dribbling, to see where other players are so he can quickly decide whether to hold the ball or pass to an open teammate.

most of the field. You will begin to spot the goalkeeper so that you can shoot past him and your unmarked teammates so that you can pass to them.

Players like Ronnie Sharp of Miami or Roy Sinclair of Seattle seem to know exactly where everyone is and just what they should do with the ball when they are dribbling. Sometimes they seem to have eyes in the back of their heads. And I have never seen a great player who did not have his visual abilities highly developed.

However, you can be sure these players did not have this ability the first time they walked on the soccer pitch (field). Seeing things at a glance must be practiced—on and off the field. The next time you are riding in a car, see how many objects, people, or colors you can spot at a quick glance while watching the road in front of you. You will be amazed at how many things you can see.

USES OF DRIBBLING

Once you have mastered the basic dribbling skills, you will find yourself falling back on them in many situations. Every player on the field will dribble sometime during a game. Some of the more common reasons for dribbling include shielding the ball from an opponent, stealing the ball from an opponent and advancing it up the field, and bypassing an opponent while in possession of the ball.

Shielding

To shield a ball from an opponent, you keep your body between the opponent and the ball. Many times in a game you will receive a ball and momentarily have no one to pass to. If your opponent is marking you tightly, it is essential that you shield the ball until help comes from your teammates. You must continually look over your shoulder so that you know where your opponent is at all times. And when he moves to steal the ball, you must quickly change your position so that you remain between him and the ball and move the ball to a new position so that he cannot tackle it or kick it away from you. What might seem like a very long time in a game because of

58

your anxiety may be only a few seconds. Therefore, along with shielding the ball it is important that you can remain cool, calm and collected. Shielding is a relatively simple skill to accomplish; keeping calm might be more difficult.

Shielding can easily be practiced with one player dribbling and another player attempting to steal the ball away. If you can shield the ball from an opponent for 30 seconds to 1 minute in a space 10 yards square, you will have ample skill to use this method in a game.

Another type of practice that I use with the Atoms is one against one in a 10-yard square with both players having a ball. You must protect your ball from the other player and at the same time attempt to kick the other player's ball or touch it while maintaining possession of yours. You are not allowed to leave your ball and run after your opponent's ball. Therefore, you are actually practicing shielding and still looking around at the same time. This will help develop your visual ability while shielding the ball.

Open-field Dribbling

It is also important to be able to dribble in an open-field condition. Many times in a game you will receive a ball and have only space and green grass in front of you. When this situation occurs, you should dribble the ball into this space as quickly as possible. This "speed" dribbling requires a slightly different style. Tight control is not so essential as moving quickly. Therefore, you push or kick the ball a longer distance in front of you and sprint up to it, rather than running with the ball right at your feet. I must caution you, however, not to push the ball any further ahead than your speed will allow if the opponent is near. And the moment your opponent starts to close in, you must then go back to tight-ball-control dribbling.

Dribbling by an Opponent

The most difficult skill of all is dribbling by an opponent. This really becomes an art with the great players; it requires a lot of skill,

Karl Minor, an Atoms forward, utilizes his body and the inside of his foot to dribble the ball around an Italian defender.

as well as deception. You must be able to run while keeping the ball within touch of both feet, to feint, and then to explode quickly in the opposite direction of your feint.

Practice running with short, choppy steps—changing direction and touching the ball on nearly every step. Once you have achieved this close dribbling control, work on your feints. It is essential to sell your feint to an opponent. Generally, you advance towards an opponent in a slow, deliberate manner, touching the ball at nearly every step. Then, when you are close to him, you feint in one direction and, if he moves with your feint, you push the ball off in the opposite direction and accelerate by the opponent.

This bypassing movement is no good unless you still have control of the ball when you have passed your opponent. Achieving a very fast burst of speed while still controlling the ball is very difficult to do. The great dribblers make it look easy, but they have put years of experience and hours and hours of practice into developing their skill.

chapter six

There are no more crucial skills in soccer than passing and kicking. Team members must be able to retain the ball among themselves until a scoring opportunity occurs, which is impossible without skillful passing capability. And when opportunities to score do arise, players must be able to take advantage of them with strong accurate kicks. Sometimes, players use kicking to get the ball out of danger near their own goal, too.

PASSING

Because soccer is a team sport, the most effective play involves a tremendous amount of passing among players. Most times, loss of the ball is due to faulty passing rather than effective ball stealing on

passing and kicking

the opponent's part. Consequently, I would have to place *passing* on the top of my "need to learn" list.

Effective passing was one reason the Los Angeles Aztecs won the North American Soccer League Championship in 1974. Team members simply passed the ball among themselves until they were able to find one of their dangerous strikers (such as Doug McMillan, NASL Rookie of the Year in 1974) alone in front of the goal. A good pass to a player like McMillan, when he's within shooting range, more times than not results in a score.

Keeping possession of the ball for as long as it takes to create a scoring opportunity is the final aim of all teams. Only a skilled passing team can achieve this aim. If you are part of a team whose members have all developed the ability to pass the ball correctly, you probably enjoy the game more and win more too.

Barry Barto (2) of Philadelphia is about to use his instep to pass the ball forward to his attacking teammate, Jim Fryatt (3).

Basic Skills

Being able to pass the ball correctly to set up a goal chance for a dangerous striker requires a great deal of practice at developing this skill. Two very important factors in successful passing are accuracy and speed.

Accuracy. The coach's cry, "pass to feet," is simple and clear. Your teammate's feet or stockings are your target. If you miss slightly, his reaction still will allow him to move into position to receive the pass, but anything wide of the target gives your opponent the advantage.

Speed of Pass. There are several factors involved in deciding the speed of your pass. The distance between you and your teammate is the most important of these. Obviously, if he is nearby, your pass can be pushed to him, but, if he is a long distance away, the ball must be driven to him, as in a low goal shot. Another consideration is your teammate's skill. If his control is bad, you must make it easy for him; even though a hard-driven pass may be the correct choice, it won't do any good if your teammate loses the ball because of poor ball control.

Types of Passes

There are many different types of passes. Only the basic passes are described below.

Inside-of-foot Pass. Using the inside of your foot is the safest and most widely used way for a beginner to pass. You use your foot like a golf putter, turning your toe out, so you have a large striking sur-

Harold Jarman of New York, partly screened by teammate Werner Roth (4), stops to make an inside-of-the-foot pass by Philadelphia defenders Tom Galati (12) and George O'Neill (11).

face; this enables you to pass with accuracy. Strike the ball in the center and follow through. You'll probably find this pass especially effective over short distances.

Remember on the inside-of-foot pass:
1. To pull your toes up as far as possible and lock your ankle;
2. To strike the ball in center; and
3. To follow through and up toward the target.

Outside-of-foot Pass. The outside-of-foot pass is more deceptive and does not require as much physical adjustment as the inside-of-foot pass. Therefore, more and more players are using this passing technique. Basically, you point your toes down and inward, and, again, lock your ankle. Strike the ball on the inside section (picture the ball as you approach it from behind divided into 3 sections—an inside, middle, and outside section) and follow through with the foot towards your target.

Remember on the outside-of-foot pass:
1. To push your toes down and lock your ankle;
2. To strike the ball on its inner third section; and
3. To follow through to the target.

Chip Pass. Many times in a game you have to pass over an opponent. This pass is called a chip pass, because you chip the ball into the air, as in a golf chip shot. In addition to getting height with this pass, you also tend to put backspin on the ball, which helps your teammate's ball control. If the pass is chipped in front of a teammate who is going to run on to the ball, the backspin will keep the ball from "running away" when it lands. Even the fastest strikers, such as Ade Coker, of the Boston Minutemen, and Keith Aqui, of the Baltimore Comets, can't catch up to most chips in front of them unless they have some backspin to keep them from running away.

The chip pass is more difficult than the first two passes. To chip a ball, the toe must be pushed downward and the ankle locked. Your approach to the ball should be somewhat from the side. Push your knee inward and cock your leg so that you strike the ball on the bottom third. After striking the ball, lean back and allow your foot to follow through in an upward motion; this will cause the ball to rise and give you the needed height or loft.

I suggest you begin using the chip pass with rolling balls coming

Bill Straub demonstrates chipping. Notice how he digs his foot underneath the ball and how he is beginning to lean back. As he follows through, the ball will rise.

67

toward you. The roll will help your height in the beginning and will help you get the proper feel for chipping.

Instep Pass. To execute the instep pass, meet the ball with your instep, pushing your toes down and locking your ankle. This technique is similar to the technique you will use for shooting the ball, but power is not so important. Do remember, however, to keep the ball low when you pass it.

Bended Pass. The *bended pass*, which is simple to execute if you have the proper technique for the instep pass, is a modern technique. If you strike the ball on the outside third (kicking right-footed), it automatically will receive a right to left spinning motion which will cause it to curve from right to left. This is an excellent pass to use when passing to your left, a pass which your teammate has to run on to. The curve will bring the ball into his run, which will make control easy for him to achieve.

The bended pass left to right necessitates striking the ball (right-footed kick) on its inner third. This imparts a spin that will cause the ball to curve to the right. Again, this is an excellent pass for someone on your right to run on to.

Gunther Netzer, of West Germany, uses the bended pass exceptionally well in getting the ball to open teammates; he can make perfect bended passes over 50 yards look easy.

Conclusion

My contention is that the real fun of the game is when your team has the ball. Then, the opponent cannot score and you can. Personally, I kind of like this advantage. I would soon dislike playing soccer if I spent every game chasing the ball from opponent to opponent.

The Atoms work every day on possession soccer. Although there are other factors than passing involved, give me 11 players who can pass well and the rest will be easy. If you can master these six different passes, you are on the way to successful possession soccer.

KICKING SKILLS

If you want "to get your kicks" in soccer, you have to become

NASL all-time leading scorer, Carlos Medetieri, passes the ball with the inside of his foot while on the run.

familiar with the different techniques of kicking a soccer ball. Whether you are shooting goals, kicking free kicks, passing, or defensively clearing the ball, your choice of technique is very important.

However, one element is common to almost every kicking technique; the instep is the part of the foot used. It seems to be perfectly shaped and is the area where you can make the hardest impact on the ball. Players who have just begun their soccer careers frequently feel they will be able to kick the ball better by striking it with their toes. This not only takes away from their power (just ask Garo Yepremian where it's best to strike any type of ball), but it also takes away from their accuracy. Once you have mastered kicking with your instep, you'll realize how much more effective it is.

Shooting Goals

Shooting goals is one of the most exciting parts of the game. We have all kicked zillions of shots on goal, before or after practice, but goals still light up the face of the shooter.

The Atoms' Roy Evans prepares his shot against Vera Cruz of Mexico. His toe is extended downward so that he will strike the ball with his instep. Note eyes on ball rather than goal.

Power and accuracy are the two important factors to remember when shooting for goal. Since a goal is only 8 feet high and 24 feet wide, the area you are shooting for is relatively small, especially when the goalkeeper stands in it. And shots over the top count for nothing. You must keep the shot low! I once had a coach who insisted that the shooter chase every shot that didn't go into the goal. I hated that rule, but we soon started concentrating on hitting the target; now I think it was a good coaching trick and helped my shooting development. Making a good impact on the ball is some kind of feeling; I can turn my back and still tell you if a shot is good or not just by listening to the sound.

I work out my goalkeepers nearly every day by kicking hundreds of shots at them. Some days my right leg almost falls off, but I enjoy every shot except those that go far astray. And it seems that they try a bit harder for every shot when the coach is shooting.

Sometimes power shots beat the goalkeeper, and other times floating balls out of his reach in the corners become winners. Extra spin on a hard shot also makes life difficult for the goalkeeper. You can get spin and curve on the ball by striking it off center either right or left, as in the bended pass. You can also make a shot dip in a downward motion. This is difficult to do to a still ball, but a bouncing ball can easily be dipped; strike the ball high up on your instep (just above where you tie your shoes) and punch through the ball: the ball will dip for you and be very difficult for the goalkeeper to stop.

You should remember the following points when shooting:

1. Kick the ball with your instep, pushing your toes down and locking your ankle;
2. Place your non-kicking foot alongside the ball (if you step in back of the ball the shot will rise);
3. Draw your kicking foot back by bending it at the knee, and then snap the foot forward (this whip gives you the power);
4. Kick through the center of the ball for all-out power;
5. Stay over the ball with the knee of the kicking foot and with the head (this time keep the shot low); and
6. Do not follow through high with the foot.

71

Stan Startzell of the Atoms shows perfect shooting form. His non-shooting foot is alongside the ball while his other leg is being cocked back for the shot. Notice Stan's eyes are on the ball so he'll know exactly where to strike it.

72

Atoms' Tom Galati shoots with such power that the follow-through lifts his non-kicking foot off the turf.

Volley

In game situations, time does not always allow you to control the ball and then kick it. Kicking the ball directly out of the air is called a volley. Volleys are used for shots on goal, defensive clearances, and lob passes. If struck on the instep, they are powerful kicks. *Volley Goal Shots.* It is possible to turn a ball kicked across the goal into a goal shot by using a volley. Face the direction the ball is coming from, place your weight on one foot (which pivots towards

73

George O'Neill of the Atoms volleys a difficult shot but still keeps it low by punching it rather than swinging through and upward.

the goal as you kick), and cock the other for the shot. You must time the kick so that you strike the ball with the instep behind the ball. Your foot actually wraps around the ball and then follows through towards the goal. To kick behind the ball, you will have to lean away from the direction of the ball.

The volley goal shot, though a difficult skill on a hard-hit ball, can be mastered through patience, persistence, and practice. However, many players, even on a professional level, feel it is smarter for them to spend their time refining the other more basic techniques than to spend long hours on such a specialized skill as the volley shot. Consequently, those, such as Paul Childs of San Jose, who do take the time to learn one of these more difficult skills become increasingly dangerous players.

Volley Kick. The volley kick is used in times of panic and urgency.

74

Derek Travis demonstrates an instep volley.

A ball landing or bouncing in the penalty area can always be turned into a goal by an alert forward. The volley kick gives a harassed defender the height and distance to get it out of danger quickly. The ball is met firmly on the instep or inside of the foot with a high follow-through. Never let the ball bounce; volley it. You can also strike the ball an easy blow for a short lob pass.

Overhead Volley. To volley a ball back over your head requires timing and a scissorslike motion with your legs, called the scissors or bicycle kick. If you are kicking the ball with your right foot, lift your left foot up first. As the left goes to the ground, the right foot scissors up and volleys the ball. You must lean backwards as you kick.

You can never tell when this shot will come in handy. I personally remember one time when a sensational overhead volley saved a national tournament game. I was coaching a college team against

Overhead volley by Philadelphia's Roy Evans in a game against Vera Cruz of Mexico.

Harvard in 1970. Somewhere around the middle of this tension-packed match, a Harvard striker on the right side of our goal hit a high, hard shot that curved toward the far corner of the net. My goalkeeper at the time was Norm Wingert, co-author of this book and currently a member of my Philadelphia club. He dived futilely towards the ball, which was well out of his reach and heading for the back of the net. At the last second, however, just before the ball was about to enter the upper left-hand corner of the net, one of my strikers, Alec Papadakis, who had come back to help out on defense, made a dramatic, leaping, overhead volley, kicking the ball up and over the crossbar a split second before it would have crossed the goal line. Alec's mastery of the overhead volley saved us that game and moved us on to the national finals that year.

You can also hit an overhead volley for a shot on goal, but instead of leaning backwards, you must fall backwards as you strike the ball. You break your fall with your hands outstretched behind you. Some players are very good at this, and, if you ever score a goal using the scissors kick, you won't forget it for a long time.
Half Volley. A half volley is hitting the ball just after it hits the ground. You short hop the ball and shoot it using the instep kick, or use the volley kick technique if you want it to clear.

chapter seven

Heading—making contact with the ball with the head—is one of the most difficult and sensational skills used in soccer. People who watch a soccer game for the first time always are amazed at how players head the ball and never seem to get hurt. Great headers, such as Atoms' striker Jim Fryatt and Dallas' Kyle Rote, have nearly perfect technique. Consequently, they are able to head in goals under terrific pressure from opponents. Rote brought Dallas into the 1973 NASL championship with a brilliant header that wound up beating the New York Cosmos in a semifinal playoff, 1-0. Another outstanding NASL header, Randy Howrton, of New York, also played in that classic play-off match in 1973. In fact, if it hadn't been for some outstanding goalkeeping by Dallas' Ken Cooper and a couple of unfortunate breaks, Howrton would have ended up tieing that play-off with a header of his own.

heading

HOW TO HEAD THE BALL

The secrets of heading are:

1. To meet the ball on your *hairline* across your forehead;
2. To punch the ball by using the neck muscles (pull your chin back);
3. To keep your eyes open and watch the ball all the way to your head.

Begin by having someone toss easy balls (underhand, since most balls in soccer come from the feet) to your head. Move behind the ball and punch it back to the thrower by pulling your chin and head back. Keep your eyes on the ball and jut your head and chin forward (not downward). Trial and error will start to get results;

Jim Fryatt shows
perfect form in
heading.

you will find that you can get a lot of power on your returns.

Once you feel comfortable, have the thrower move to one side or the other after he throws the ball. Get behind the ball, turn to face the thrower, and punch the header to him. At no time do you change your style or place of contact. By arching your back like an archer's bow, you can get additional power.

The final step in heading is learning to jump and head with the same power. The form and technique are exactly the same. The secret is to jump early and hang in the air momentarily while punching the ball. Most beginners jump into the ball rather than behind the ball. When they jump into the ball, they lose both power and accuracy.

Jumping, hanging, eyes on the ball. Fryatt against Ireland's Finn Harps does it all!

The ability to jump above the defender and head crosses to team-mates is a specialty of Atoms' Jim Fryatt (9).

Practice jumping straight up and bringing your heels up in back of you to your buttocks. This jumping form will help you hang longer in the air. Once you have mastered this form, then have someone throw the ball above your head. Jump, hang, and butt it back to the thrower. This timing will take practice, but once you get the feel, good heading soon will follow.

TYPES OF HEADING

Basically, three types of heading are required in soccer. They

Heading the ball down is important when heading the ball for goal. Here, Jim Fryatt heads one past Claude Campos of Rochester.

include heading for goals, heading passes to teammates, and heading balls out of danger in front of your goal (clearing).

Heading for Goals

When heading for goals, both power and accuracy are important. You generally attempt to knock the ball down. The goalkeeper has much more difficulty making a save near his feet. Also, there's no way you can hit the ball under the goal, no matter how hard you strike it with your head; so, if you hit the ball down, you can be sure it won't miss the goal unless you hit it wide. On the other hand, if

83

you head the ball upwards while going for the goal, there's a good chance it will end up going over its mark.

Passing with the Head

Heading spinning balls and balls that are coming at different speeds to a teammate requires great skill. The technique is somewhat similar to goal shooting, except you don't need the same amount of power. You must take the speed or spin off the ball (by cushioning it) and head it on to your teammate all in one motion so he can easily control it. The key is looking where you want the pass to go; posi-

Jim Fryatt, the Atoms' famous target player, heads one down to teammate Andy Provan (10), an effective attacking move.

Clearing the ball on defense requires heading the ball upward. Here Fryatt, in dark uniform, clears a corner kick from the Finn Harps of Ireland.

tion yourself so that you can nod your head in the direction you want your pass to travel.

Clearance Heading

Clearance heading is used on high balls coming in to the penalty box. Since all goals are scored within this territory, it is urgent that all balls are headed out of this danger zone. When heading a ball clear of the goal, try for height and distance. If possible, also get direction; head toward the nearest touchline. To get height, it is vital to strike the bottom section of the ball. You use the same technique, but hitting the lower part of the ball will cause the ball to go up. As a defender, you must get to a high ball first. If a forward is allowed to make first contact, you may end up picking the ball out of your net.

IMPROVING HEADING ABILITY

In the teaching of many soccer skills, a pendulum ball can be quite helpful. (A pendulum ball is simply a regulation soccer ball with a swivel mounted on the top of the ball; a string is attached to the swivel, and the ball is hung from a horizontal fixture approximately 20 feet high.) Heading is one of the skills this ball swinging on a rope can assist in developing. I have used the pendulum ball extensively in working with beginners and have gotten excellent results in developing good heading style.

Suspend the pendulum ball so that it is at head height while you are standing behind the ball. Start by punching the ball forward, and, as the ball swings back to your head, punch it again or catch it. If you punch the ball on the wrong part of your forehead, the ball will go off in a sideways direction, but, when you meet the ball properly, the ball will swing directly forward and return to where you are standing. This will help you develop a sense of timing.

You can also use a pendulum ball to gauge your power. When you punch the ball, punch it strongly. The distance the ball swings away from you will give you an indication of the power that you got behind the ball.

When you can control the ball at head height, raise it slightly, so that a jump is needed before heading. You must learn to jump and hang behind the ball before punching it. With a stationary pendulum ball, you will learn to do this by trial and error. You will not be able to get any power or to punch the ball away from you if you jump directly into the ball; it will simply go up and jump around on the string.

After you have developed the proper technique, then you might bring an opponent in to fight with you for the ball. See if you can hit five headers first. This kind of jumping and riding an opponent's charge is very similar to what happens in a game.

Practicing heading with a pendulum ball setup is also good for

86

Even great headers like Jim Fryatt cannot rely on heading alone.
Here Fryatt is shown shooting a difficult shot—he has had to reach
for the ball.

developing your jump. Obviously, the more you practice, the better
your timing will become and the stronger and higher the jump,
itself.

Once your style is established, the last step, of course, is learning
to use heading on flighted balls. The best way to do this is to practice heading balls that are either thrown or kicked to you.

I do want to point out that pendulum-ball practice is not the only
way to develop heading techniques. Our great header, Jim Fryatt,
one of the best headers in the world, has never used a pendulum
ball. I have talked at great length with Jim about heading, and he
concludes that the timing of the jump, the courage to fight off opponents' bumps, and the ability to keep the eyes open and snap the
neck muscles into the ball all contribute to heading ability.

Winning the ball off an opponent is no small competitive

challenge. Sticking your head into the crowd while going for goals requires courage of the highest standard. Good headers go to the ball; they don't wait for it to come to them. The men who score goals by heading are courageous men who can outjump opponents and use good technique under pressure.

Derek Trevis, an Atoms defender, has jumped early and Rochester player cannot get up to the ball as Trevis' arm prevents. However, such errors of judgment cannot always be avoided.

HEADING IN AMERICAN SOCCER

I am of the opinion that heading is the weakest skill in American soccer. Every place I go, I see players squeezing their eyes shut, stretching their necks out, and jumping up into the ball, rather than keeping their eyes open, jumping behind the ball, and withdrawing their heads so they can punch the ball by extending their head forward. This is a bit shocking, since most of our players jump very well as a result of exposure to basketball. As in every other soccer skill, there is no magic way to acquire heading ability other than constant repetition and practice. When practicing heading, bring in the opponent as quickly as possible, since it is quite different to head a ball over the head of an opponent or to jump up ahead of him than it is to head a ball without any competition. As I have mentioned earlier, heading is a beautiful skill when executed properly, and many great goals are scored every year by the use of the head.

chapter eight

I often compare a team to an orchestra. An orchestra is made up of individual musical ability blended with other talents, directed by a leader. The final aim is to have each individual give of himself to create the symphony. A soccer team is similar in almost every respect. A good team needs 11 players with specific talents. They must understand each other in every way, which comes with daily practice in small groups.

The evolution of team tactics or strategy requires the combined effort of players and coach. The coach must analyze each player's talents and strong points and place them in a position where they can utilize their abilities to the utmost. Goal scorers are most difficult to find or develop. When a coach finds a player with a knack for scoring goals, he would be foolish to place the player in midfield

soccer strategy

or defense. But if a player is a good passer of the ball, he has to be in the midfield, since this is where creative passing is necessary. Other players make excellent tacklers or winners of the ball; they are needed in the defense. Even though every player must be an all-around player, his individual strengths will still show. It is the coach's job to find the correct place in the team for every player.

Once a balanced team is formed, three types of tactics are employed by soccer players in a game—individual tactics, group tactics, and team tactics.

INDIVIDUAL TACTICS

Individual tactics vary according to which team has the ball.

The player finds himself in many awkward positions. Here, Karl Minor, Atom forward, collides with three Italian Army players.

Whenever you have the ball in your possession, anything that you do to start the attack requires an individual tactic. For instance, you could try to dribble by an opponent or you could decide to shield the ball until a teammate runs into position for a pass. If the other team has the ball, someone on your team must attempt to win the ball back for your team by tackling (stealing) the ball from your opponent, or a player must defend closely enough to the opponent so that it will become difficult for him to make an advancing pass.

Scoring goals becomes difficult whenever the defender stays between his opponent and the goal.

Defending

Defending against an opponent or opponents requires special techniques. Not too long ago it was thought that only specialists should do the defending. However, today each player must defend as well as attack, so defensive tactics must be learned.

If your man (the man you are defending) doesn't have the ball: Stay between your man and the goal. Look at the ball and your man. Never let your man receive a pass behind you. Be ready to intercept any pass made to your man. Stay close to your man.

On the other hand, if your man has the ball: Stay between him and the goal. Look at the ball (don't watch him). Stay low to the ground and on your toes. Don't go for the ball unless you are 100 percent positive you can get it. Force him to the side (away from the goal or his best foot). Tackle the ball whenever possible. Feint and keep the opponent off balance.

Tackling

Tackling the ball away from an opponent is a technique that must be learned. To tackle the ball really means to block the ball and then pull it away from the opponent. The front block tackle is most commonly used. First, concentrate on the ball. When you feel it is far enough in front of your opponent, move quickly in for the tackle. Your tackling foot assumes the same position as when you are making an inside-of-foot pass. You will need this broad surface for your block. Your weight is pushed down on the tackling foot, making it firm and supported by your body weight. The moment you feel the impact from your opponent, either kicking or tackling the ball, you must react and pull the ball away from him. Obviously, he will be thinking about doing the same, so speed of thought and reflex is most important.

Defenders must be cool and patient. Beginners always want the ball immediately and end up tackling the air as the opponent pulls the ball away from the swinging foot. Wait for the ball to come away from your opponent; then steal it. As long as you are between him and the goal he is not dangerous. He can't shoot the ball through you.

The safest way for you to go for the ball is while your teammate backs you up. A coach works hard with his team to make the players cover each other on defense. I have appointed one man (our captain, Derek Trevis) to cover all players defensively. It is his job to be the last man to beat before the enemy gets to goalkeeper Bob Rigby. Two men working together to recover a ball, however, is not an individual tactic; it is a group tactic.

GROUP TACTICS

When two or more teammates play together in either an attacking or defending role, they are utilizing group tactics. If you have the ball and your teammate runs into a position so that you can pass to him when an opponent gets too close, you and your teammate have utilized an excellent group tactic. When more than one teammate runs into position, your group tactics become even stronger. A defense is also much stronger when players work in pairs or threes around the ball. An attacking player who dribbles by one defender is not free with another defender, or two, in position to challenge him.

Jim Fryatt (in white) shooting on goal. Notice how his toe is extended downward.

Here, Andy Provan, the Atoms' high-scoring forward, places his kicking foot alongside the ball and prepares his shot.

Players soon recognize teammates' strengths and weaknesses and learn to utilize them in group tactics. A good example of this is the combination of Fryatt and Provan, who played on our championship team in 1973. Though both players are high goal scorers, they are complete opposites. Fryatt is a tough player, excellent header, and most effective with an opponent literally hanging on him; he rarely dribbles by an opponent but makes goals for players around him. Provan, on the other hand, enjoys dribbling by people nearly as much as he enjoys scoring goals. He likes space and avoids physical contact whenever he can. These players, so different in temperament and style, have learned to blend their talents, and they

96

are undoubtedly the best one-two punch in the NASL. This is one small example of team development and aids a coach's strategy tremendously. Obviously, these players have developed a deep understanding of each other in practice and in games.

If you were able to isolate play action of the better teams, you would find players constantly making pairs by running to aid each other. It is impossible for the entire 11 players on a team to be totally involved all at once. Rather, 2 or 3 members of the team are totally involved, and, as the ball progresses either forward, backward, or sideways, other members on the team become linked together into new playing units. This type of giving yourself for the benefit of the team is the essential ingredient in small group tactics.

I place much emphasis on small group tactics in our practices and would advocate this type of training for youth teams. Eleven against 11 games (scrimmages) don't allow enough ball contacts for each player. The moment the numbers are reduced, every player is totally involved. When the small group play becomes smooth and efficient, one can then be assured that the players will play well as a team and are ready to employ total team tactics.

TEAM TACTICS

Systems of Play

Soccer is a team game, and I can't stress the need for teamwork enough. This involves definite cooperation between the coach and the players. Team tactics are related to systems of play. The coach must analyze his players and decide what system of play is the best to use. It is my opinion that there are no magic systems of play but that games are won or lost on individual and group tactics. Each team must have a numerical posture, however. The coach decides this posture on the basis of the players he has available to him. He must then develop this system on the blackboard and on the practice field.

Almost every professional team in the world utilizes at least four players on defense, a minimum of two at midfield, and a minimum of two as attackers, plus, of course, the goalkeeper. This totals nine players. The coach now has the choice of placing the remaining two players wherever it would seem to be to the team's advantage. If both of them are placed as forwards, the system of play is 4-2-4 (defenders, midfielders, and attackers, respectively). If the two are placed at midfield, the system becomes 4-4-2, which is heavily defensive. Changes during the season or in a game are made to generate more attack or more defense, whichever is required at the time.

However, in no way should these numbers restrict any player or group of players. Every player must feel free to defend or attack, depending on circumstances. Don't restrict your individual contribution to the team by playing only the position to which you are assigned.

But every player does have to have a clear understanding of his and his teammates' responsibilities in a particular system. Once this is established the players can help each other. The coach must set up practices to develop every aspect of team play. Defense, midfield, and attack should be broken down into small pieces and developed. And players must discuss with each other how to solve every problem. Small groups should practice coordination among each other, and do's and don'ts should be established and worked on until they are clearly understood.

Specific Team Tactics

In some playing situations—corner kicks, free kicks, and throw-ins—set plays called restarts are used. The Atoms practice these plays (and the defense against them) nearly every day, because many goals are scored during a season by using them.

One way *you* may be involved in a restart is if you have to throw the ball back into play from the touchline. According to the rules, the throw-in must take place at the spot where the ball went out of play. You must throw the ball with both hands from directly behind the head, and both feet must remain on the ground until the ball is thrown.

The main objective on a throw-in is to maintain possession. To get the ball in play quickly, throw it to your teammate's feet, so he can control it quickly and start playing possession soccer again. You can use one of three throwing techniques to put the ball back into play—the parallel feet throw, the split feet throw, or the running drag throw.

In the *parallel feet throw-in,* stand with both feet together, facing the field of play. Place the hands behind the ball and take the ball behind your head. Use an arm-whipping throwing motion and release the ball after it has passed the top of your head. Follow through toward your target. You can get additional distance by arching your back for additional whipping motion to get more power.

In the *split feet throw-in,* face the field and place one foot by the touchline and the other foot back a stride. Use the exact same throwing motion, but, when straightening up your back, slide the toe of your back foot forward along the ground without lifting it until it is parallel with your stationary foot. Some players feel this throw-in is more comfortable and helps them get additional distance.

The *running throw-in* should only be used to throw a long distance. Begin several steps back from the touchline. Run towards the field of play while taking the ball back to throwing position. Plant one foot at the touchline and use the split feet throwing technique. The run will put additional momentum behind the throw-in. Steve Bauman, Miami's rookie winger, can throw a ball legally halfway across the field. This is a good weapon when his team receives a throw-in on the attacking third of the field, because he can throw the ball directly in front of the goal where his teammates are positioned to head the ball into the goal.

Beginning players should use the parallel feet throw-in technique, because the rules award the opposing team the ball if the throw-in is illegal (lifting one of your feet, throwing with one hand, stepping on the field of play). A legal throw-in assures your team of a good chance of keeping possession, so don't complicate matters.

The Final Step

Once the coach feels that his team is working as a team, he must arrange practice games to help develop the team further. Team meetings should be held after each game to discuss problems, and in succeeding practices, the mistakes should be ironed out. No detail is too small, and every player should continually analyze his role and work hard in practice to improve his performance.

Harmony on and off the field is another important ingredient in good teamwork. An unselfish approach to the game is the best attitude a group of players can develop. The Atoms, in 1973, had a genuinely deep feeling for each other; every man was playing for the team. The individual efforts were tremendous, and stardom came out of our success for some players. But every man gave of himself unselfishly.

It is important for you to understand that teamwork is the end result of individuals functioning as individuals but blending their talents with others in a smooth organized fashion. As each individual improves his abilities, the team will improve.

SOCCER STYLES

In countries where soccer has been played enthusiastically over a long period of time, actual playing styles have developed. These are somewhat influenced by weather conditions. In South America, for example, where the weather is very hot, the players have learned to conserve energy by playing more skillfully at a slower pace. It is easy to recognize that the heat will not allow 90 minutes of very fast running. Therefore, most South American players are very skillful but lack fighting power.

England's weather, on the other hand, is cold and wet. And English players play at a much faster pace than the South Americans. The players must run to keep warm, and the rain makes the fields heavy, which requires added leg strength and fighting power. Both styles are effective when played properly, and both are necessary for success in their climatic conditions.

The 1974 world champion team from West Germany combined South American skill and English fighting power. They played very skillfully when they had the ball, putting together 20 or more passes at one time. The ball never stopped, and the way they kept possession was a performance. The players were constantly moving and interchanging positions. The defenders all took turns in coming forward and getting involved in the attack. But, when they lost possession, they looked like angry men insulted by the opponent who took it away. They chased and fought until they got the ball back; and then, suddenly, the anger would subside and they would appear happy again, light-footing back on attack.

Strategy is constantly changing and innovations are constantly coming to our attention. But analysis of the new developments shows that the real secret is the individual player. Players today are just better than players in the past. They are more skillful and better prepared physically.

I often wonder what our style will be in North America. I am sure fitness will play a major role. Our players are courageous and know the value of hard training. Our skill level is low now but improving at an unbelievable pace, and our tactical development will improve as the coaches and players improve. We will soon know more about our soccer style, because a U.S. team is already being prepared for the 1978 World Cup in Argentina. Our coach, Dettmar Cramer, is a soccer expert and a master at team preparation. Can you imagine the United States some day winning a world championship that the entire world is competing fiercely for. I can't wait.

chapter nine

The one man on a soccer field who can use his hands is the goal-keeper. This one player is allowed such a great advantage, because he has to stop the ball from going into a goal 8 feet high and 24 feet wide—a pretty tough task considering some shots are going 80 miles an hour.

With such a large area to protect from bulletlike shots, often spinning down (or away) from him, it is no surprise that a good goalkeeper must have lightning-fast reflexes and a sure pair of hands. However, I have seen goalkeepers who are not so quick or sure-handed become outstanding by developing proper goalkeeping skills and playing with a strong desire to succeed, using both their heart and their head.

Even if you never have thought of being a goalkeeper, you should

goalkeeping

try the position some day just for the fun of it and to see what it is really like being the last man on defense in front of those wide-open nets. All attacking players—and in today's modern soccer *everyone* should be an attacker (as well as a defender)—would like to know what is going through the opposing goalkeeper's mind. By spending some time in the nets, you are likely to gain some understanding of how a goalkeeper thinks and might react. This is sure to be a big plus in your favor when playing out on the field.

You might also find that you enjoy the position and have good potential as a "keeper." Both the Atoms' goalkeepers, Bob Rigby and Norm Wingert, played in other spots until their last couple of years in high school. In fact, I have known some fine goalkeepers who didn't begin playing there until they were in college. Don't let

103

Catch ball at highest point, eyes on ball. Note that the goalkeeper's hands are behind the ball and that he will catch it with his fingers, not with his palms.

this fool you though; the goalkeeper, like the rest of the players on a soccer field, must master several important skills.

CATCHING THE BALL

Since you have the tremendous advantage of being allowed to use your hands, make full use of them by catching the ball whenever possible. Trying to hold on to rocketlike shots isn't easy for anyone, but learning to catch the ball correctly helps. The first thing to remember is to keep both hands slightly behind the ball. This prevents the ball from slipping through your hands even on hard shots.

The ball is caught with your fingers, not at all with your palms. (If the ball hits the palms of your hands, it's likely to bounce free.) Spread your fingers apart. As the shot hits them, grab the ball securely and give with the shot slightly, which will make it easier to hold onto.

Hard shots that are held save dozens of rebound goals every year on all levels of play. You can make important saves and hold onto them, too, if you practice catching the ball the way I just mentioned.

However, even the best goalkeepers fail to hold onto some shots. Therefore, you also should make an effort to get your body behind the ball whenever possible, no matter how hard or soft it has been hit. This will at least assure you of stopping the shot. It also gives you the option of catching the ball against your chest on shots coming at that level. Many goalkeepers prefer catching the ball like this,

Get body behind ball.

Pull back into chest. Protect yourself and ball.

especially in a crowd of players, since they feel it provides them with the best possible way of protecting the ball and keeping it from being jarred loose.

High Balls

One of your biggest advantages as a goalkeeper is being able to get high lobs and crosses before all other players, since you are allowed to use your hands. Catch these balls at the top of a jump with your arms fully extended above your head. When there are attacking players around, you will find it necessary frequently to come toward the ball to catch it at the highest point above your head that you can. But don't wait for the ball to drop and come to you, because someone else may head it in for a goal. There's no need for this ever to happen if you learn to catch high balls properly.

Low Balls

Many goalkeepers find shots on the ground somewhat easier to handle than those high hard ones hit above their heads. Remember, if shots come on the ground, get your body behind the ball. The slowest rolling shot can slip through the best goalkeeper's hands on a rare occasion. If you have your body behind the ball you can be

Catch ball at its highest point. Fingers spread, both hands behind ball. Arms fully extended.

sure it's not getting by, even if you momentarily get butterfingers.

On hard shots or on wet days, take the ball with one knee on the ground and the other leg pointing slightly sideways, but be sure not to leave a wide gap between your legs that the ball could slip through if you misplay it.

If a shot or a pass that went off its mark is rolling fairly slowly towards the goal, go to meet it. A smart goalkeeper gets easy rolling balls as fast as possible and distributes them to his teammates. This takes your team off defense and puts it on the attack. If you're quick enough, you can catch some of the other team's players out of position and really help open up things for your own offense. On the other hand, if you stand around waiting for a slow ball to come to you, a forward might dart from a position on the field where you hadn't noticed him.

If possible, don't drop down on your knee to play slow rolling shots. Instead, remain standing and bend from your waist and knees to pick the ball up with both your hands and body behind the ball. There are two advantages in taking the ball this way. First, if the ball hits something on the ground and squirts off to the side, you can easily take a step or two and still make the save. If you're down on the ground, a ball like this might go beyond your reach and get away. Secondly, if you take the ball in a standing position you'll be able to get it off to an open teammate without the delay of getting up off the ground. The split second it takes to get up may be all the time someone from the other team needs to run over and cover your once-free teammate.

Diving Saves

As a goalkeeper, you are sure to find yourself (if you haven't already) in the position of having to save a shot coming to the side of you too fast to get to using normal means. You will be forced to make a sideways diving save in these situations.

In making a diving save, use your legs as launching pads to push your body out towards the spot (be it the lower corner or the upper corner of the goal) where the ball is headed. If you are diving to your right, your right foot should be the one you are mainly pushing

Pushing off with the outside foot is a basic fundamental for all dives a goalkeeper has to make.

from. Going to your left, your left foot should supply most of the push. Your entire body should hurtle into the air sideways with your arms extending out towards that point where you will catch the ball.

If your dive is strong, you may get close enough to the shot to catch it up against your chest, where you can quickly cradle it with your hands and protect it from being jarred loose upon hitting the ground. But many times the shot will be too far from you to do this. Then you will have to catch the ball with your hands alone. Be sure

Get body down and behind ball; control ball with both hands. Break fall with hips.

to catch the ball properly, according to the method previously described, so you will consistently hold it.

If the shot is low, go down on your side; all you have to be sure of is to get to the ground before the ball is by you. Being on the ground a second before the ball gets there is perfectly all right; the ball will simply come into the wall of your body.

After you have caught the ball on a diving ground shot or a diving shot you have plucked out of the air, pull the ball into your body and up against your chest. This prevents the diving balls you snatch in flight from being jarred loose when you hit the ground. A loose ball in front of a goal with the 'keeper on the ground is a great opportunity for a hungry forward to score.

Another way of handling midair saves is to take the ball, securely within your grasp, to the ground first, pulling it in slightly so that you end up landing on the ball.

My personal feeling is that you should try making aerial saves using both of the methods described. After awhile, you probably will find yourself more comfortable and getting better results with one or the other, and you'll prefer making midair diving saves that one way. With enough practice, midair saves will become a natural reaction for you.

PUNCHING AND DEFLECTING

Sometimes, on high or wide shots, you may find yourself heavily harassed by players from the other team and/or unable to get both hands cleanly on the ball for a catch. As a last resort, you may have to punch or deflect the ball away.

Punching and deflecting should be used only when absolutely necessary. If you catch the ball, you assure your team of having possession; but punching or deflecting the ball puts it up for grabs. If you should deflect the ball out of bounds, as you sometimes must do, the other team is guaranteed of staying on the attack.

On those occasions when you must punch or deflect the ball though, it is important that you do it correctly to take the pressure off your own goal and yourself as a 'keeper, at least momentarily.

Punching

You will punch the ball usually on high lobs or crosses in the goal area when a number of other players, particularly those from the other team, are blocking your way, so that a clean catch is impossible. Evaluate the situation around you as you approach your takeoff spot so that you can decide a few seconds ahead of time

111

Atoms' all-pro goalkeeper, Bob Rigby, shows his great flexibility after diving for a shot off the foot of Boston's John Coyne.

whether you will be able to catch the ball or if you will be forced to punch it.

It is important to make this decision ahead of time, because you must draw one or both fists back into the chest to prepare for a successful punch.

If you have decided it will be necessary to make a punch, *make sure you are facing the ball in such a way that the ball is coming directly at you.* This makes timing your jump for the ball much easier. When you take off in the air to meet the ball, draw back one or both fists into your chest. The choice of whether to use one or

(Facing page) Go into a crowd, jump, hang, and punch. Keep eyes on ball.

both fists together depends on how you personally feel most comfortable and get the best results. Most goalkeepers start out by using both fists together. When making a fist, keep your thumb outside the rest of your hand. If you don't, you're liable to end up with a cracked or broken thumb when you make good contact.

Just as in catching the ball, you want to make sure you meet the ball at the top of your jump. While on your way to that peak, your fists should be soaring up and out, away from your chest, so your arms are almost fully extended when your fists meet the ball.

As you punch the ball simultaneously with both fists, direct it up and out, away from yourself and the goal. If the ball is coming directly at you, which it should be since you always want to have your body and sight directly in line with the ball as it approaches, the power of your punch combined with the force of the ball rebounding off your fists should send the ball well out of danger for at least the moment at hand. This will give you and your defense time to regroup.

Deflecting

There are sure to be times in a game when, no matter how well you dive, a shot will be just too difficult to catch or punch. It may be out of reach or coming down right around the crossbar. In these situations, try to deflect the ball (change its direction) so that it goes wide or over the top of the crossbar.

In most cases, a well-executed deflection does and should give up a corner kick. As a last resort, this is better than having the ball roll free within a few yards of your own goal. Here, an attacker will have an easy time putting the ball by you, since you will most likely be on the ground and out of position. A corner kick gives you and the rest of your teammates time to get set and in position for whatever the other team may try.

Diving Deflections. On diving deflections, try to meet the ball with the palm of your hand. It is important to remember that you merely are trying to *meet* the ball in an effort to get the ball wide of the goal. You are *not* trying to hit the ball. If you do hit it, you only are increasing the chances of the ball staying in play and being knocked in for a goal. If you are unable to get your palm on the ball, you will have to try and deflect it wide with your fingertips.

As in punching, you may use one or both hands to deflect the ball. Most goalkeepers like to use both hands if possible. However, if the shot is too far from your reach, you will find you can extend yourself slightly further by going for the ball with a single hand. This makes saving the shot a riskier task, since it easily can slip above or below the limited surface of a single palm. But, at times, you may have no other choice than to take this chance. The dive itself, in deflecting the ball wide, should be made the same way as if you were going to catch the ball.

Deflections Over the Crossbar. To deflect a ball over the crossbar, you use techniques similar to those used in punching and diving deflections. To begin with, turn your entire body in the direction the ball is coming from, so the ball will be coming in to you, making it easier to time your deflection. Begin your leap as the ball comes down towards you and the crossbar; try to meet the ball at the height of the crossbar or slightly above. The deflection itself is made with the palms and fingers; as you meet the ball (usually with a single hand on this type of deflection), push it up and over the crossbar.

If a cross from the side must be deflected, you will find it easier and more effective to deflect the ball with the hand farthest from the goal line. For instance, if you are facing to your right, your left hand should be used in making the deflection. If you find it awkward deflecting the crosses over the bar using this method, use two hands for awhile, but keep practicing the other way. As you mature as a goalkeeper, you'll find this just as natural, less risky, and more effective.

CUTTING A SHOOTER'S ANGLE

As a coach, I am often surprised at how many young goalkeepers know little or nothing about "cutting down a shooter's angle," giving him as little goal to shoot at as possible. It may sound funny or

Atoms' goalkeeper, by using his open hand, goes high in the air to tip ball over the crossbar.

even impossible to you that where you position yourself determines how much goal a forward will have to shoot at. But it's true.

If an attacker is fairly far away from the goal (let's say 15 yards or more), no matter where he is coming from, your best position for stopping his shot is directly on a line drawn between him and the middle of the goal. If you are approaching a potential shooter from the middle of the goal, you will give him an equal amount of the goal to shoot at both to your left and to your right. In any other position, you give him more goal to shoot at on one side or the other. You don't want to give an attacker any extra advantage like that no matter how good you are at making diving saves. So always be careful as the ball changes positions on the field—if it is within shooting range—that your position also changes, so that you keep that constant imaginary straight line between the ball, yourself, and the middle of the goal.

Also, you give a player less goal to shoot at if you come off the goal line and out at the man. The further you come off the center of your goal line straight out at the attacker, the less area of the goal he will have to shoot at. If you come all the way out until you are on top of him, it will be impossible for him to shoot the ball by you and at the goal. He no longer has any goal to shoot at because your body now is directly in front of him and the entire goal.

Of course, no attacker will wait until you are right on top of him to shoot. However, the further you are out of the goal, in a straight line between the center of the goal and the ball, the less area of the goal you are conceding to an attacker.

There is one slight disadvantage to coming out of the goal like this: It becomes possible for the attacker to chip the ball over your head and into the goal. However, a chip like this in an actual game is extremely difficult even for the most advanced player. Therefore, whenever possible, it is wise to play at least two or three steps in front of the goal line.

If a single man begins to move in on you and it looks like he will soon be shooting, you should start moving directly at him in line with the center of the goal. Be on your toes as you move out so that you will be set to react in either direction the moment he shoots.

BREAKAWAYS

Breakaways (balls that have broken through a team's defense) are the most difficult shots for a goalkeeper to stop. To stop breakaways, you must come off your goal line and give the forward as little goal as possible to shoot at. If you watch top American professionals, such as Ken Cooper, of the Dallas Tornado, or the Atoms' Bob Rigby, you'll see they begin moving straight toward a forward on a breakaway, as soon as he is within 20 yards of the goal.

You should do the same thing. Move toward the man quickly and on your toes. However, make sure you still have complete control over your body so that you will be able to dive to either side, if necessary, when the attacker shoots. Chances are the attacker will shoot while you are between him and the goal.

However, if you should get within four or five strides of him and he still hasn't shot, prepare to slide into the ball sideways. Your body should hit the ground so that the length of it is between the goal and the man with the ball. Since you will be moving, your momentum will help carry you into the ball. And, since the ball itself will be rolling forward, it will be headed straight for your grasp. The ideal time to begin your dive is when the attacker has just pushed the ball in front of him and temporarily out of reach. Then he can't nip the ball under your body during the split second you are off the ground at the beginning of your slide. If you time the slide perfectly, you can snatch the ball onto your chest just before the attacker has a chance to touch it.

GOAL KICKS

All goalkeepers should practice goal kicks. This is part of the position's responsibility. If you see a goalkeeper who can't kick a ball properly you know he is inexperienced as a 'keeper. Practice kicking balls out of the penalty box to players 20 to 40 yards away. Accuracy is most important.

DISTRIBUTION

Ball distribution is another skill often neglected by 'keepers,

118

especially younger ones. By distributing the ball wisely, you can get your offense moving in high gear the split second you release the ball. I have seen goalkeepers actually turn themselves into effective offensive players through smart, quick distribution of the ball.

Basically, there are three ways to distribute the ball. The most common way—probably the one you first learned—is by kicking. The other two methods are rolling and throwing the ball. Any professional goalkeeper, no matter where he plays in the world, will tell you that rolling and throwing are the surest ways to keep possession of the ball and guarantee your team the attack. By insuring safe distribution to a teammate, you will deny the opponent any chance of a goal, at least for a temporary period.

Punting or Dropkicking

The major positive result of kicking is that it gets the ball out of your defensive end of the field quickly. You may either dropkick or punt the ball football-style. I suggest you practice both to see which gives you greater distance and accuracy. Practice will also build your power and timing, which should help to continually lengthen your kicks.

If you find you are not kicking the ball very far out of your own end of the field, I suggest you use rolling and throwing as your major means of distribution. Save kicking for those times when all your teammates are covered by the opposition or when the opposition has mounted a prolonged attack and you feel your defense needs a few moments to reorganize themselves and get in position.

On the other hand, if your kicks cover a long distance, use them frequently to try to catch your opponents off guard in the hope they might misjudge or misplay the ball and allow your forwards to take off on a quick attack.

Rolling the Ball

If one of your teammates is clearly free and within 15 or 20 yards of you, you should distribute the ball by rolling it to him. If you roll

119

the ball as if you were bowling, bending low with an underarm swing, it will be easy for your teammate to control and you can be assured, with some practice, of near-perfect accuracy.

Throwing

Goalkeepers also distribute the ball by throwing it, using one of two different styles. They use a baseball-type throw for shorter distances and an overhand still-arm toss for longer throws.

Most American goalkeepers have little problem developing a good baseball-style throw with a soccer ball. Make sure that your throw is overhand, to insure accuracy, and that you keep the ball at head level or below when throwing. By throwing like this, you will be able to release the ball quickly and accurately and get it speedily to an open teammate up to 35 yards away. Of course, if you are not fully grown and developed, your throws will not be as far, but you still will be able to distribute the ball effectively. You will find this method especially effective in getting the ball to teammates on the side of the field opposite from where you have just made a save or picked up a loose ball. If you look for them immediately, they will be wide open.

You probably will find the overhand stiff-arm throw more effective in long tosses, and it can be used as effectively as the baseball throw for shorter distribution with practice. You make the throw as its name implies. Keep your throwing arm stiff, with the ball encircled partially by your hand and wrist. Start the throw back near the side of your knee, and, as you come through with the toss, be sure to come straight overhand while continuing to keep your arm straight. The sooner you release the ball, the higher the throw will be. But don't let the ball go too high, or you will reduce your chances of catching the opposition's defense off guard.

COMMUNICATION

Your final responsibility as a goalkeeper is communicating with your teammates throughout the game. As a goalkeeper, you are in the unique position of being the only player on the field who constantly can see the whole game developing in front of you. By paying close attention to what is going on, you give timely help to teammates who do not have as clear a view of the developing play. A goalkeeper who can help alert one of his defenders about an uncovered attacker in a dangerous position or who can tell a teammate in trouble with the ball where to pass to is a big asset to his club. It also is your responsibility as the goalkeeper to position your teammates when they are forming a wall in front of an opposition free kick.

Of course, no matter what type of instruction or warning you give, it must be shouted loudly and distinctly, so that your teammates will be able to react immediately and take full advantage of your advice. You must also learn to make clear, distinct calls for balls you are taking, so that teammates will move out of the way. Most goalkeepers call "keeper!" A goalkeeper who communicates *at the proper times* can make his teammates more effective players.

chapter ten

A new, exciting, slightly different form of soccer has been rapidly growing in popularity in recent years—indoor soccer. Depending on where you live, you may never have heard of it, but it is one of the most popular winter sports in the Soviet Union. And, in some of the colder parts of our country, where the weather makes playing outdoors nearly impossible in the wintertime, indoor soccer is gaining popularity among colleges, amateur leagues, and professionals, too.

REASONS FOR INDOOR SOCCER

Indoor soccer is played with a small team at a hockey rink,

indoor soccer

gymnasium, or armory. The thing I like about the game is that the fans have an opportunity to see up close the tremendous skill that a soccer player possesses. It is my feeling that, because of the vastness of our stadiums, many times spectators are too far away to appreciate what is going on down on the field. In indoor soccer, this is definitely not true. The spectators are right on top of the play and can hear the thuds of the tackles and shots and observe the finesse of the player.

For the past two seasons, in the North American Soccer League, teams such as St. Louis, San Jose, Toronto, Atlanta, New York, Miami, Dallas, and Philadelphia have been playing test games to establish a standard set of rules that will make the new game an exciting one for the fans as well as a productive one for the development of professional players. As part of this program, Philadelphia hosted the Russian National Army Team in a major event in the Spectrum, Philadelphia's outstanding hockey arena. Over 14,000 spectators enthusiastically witnessed their first indoor soccer game on a professional level. The media in Philadelphia spoke very highly of the game and, speaking from a coach's point of view, it was one of my most exciting athletic experiences.

Since the Russians were far superior to our American players in skill, they finally prevailed on the scoreboard at the end. However, for the first two periods the game was evenly contested, since our players marked them very tightly and did a great job in the offensive area in getting goals. Our goalkeeper, Bob Rigby, was simply

Philly's George Seiga (10) and Bobby Smith (3) look on with relief as teammate Bob Rigby shows perfect form in snatching the ball to his midsection while making a diving save indoors.

124

outstanding in this game, and, for the first time, many of our fans really saw his capabilities.

Not only is this game popular and fun to watch, but also it solves a problem soccer players in North America have. Because of the tremendous refinement of skills required of the player, soccer requires almost year-round practice and competition. Since soccer is a relatively new professional sport in this country, players' experience has been to play a short high school or college season of three or four months and go on to another sport. I am not against this concept, but I am certain that there is no way a young player can possibly develop his talent for soccer in this short time. Professional league seasons are also too short at the present time. I believe the U.S. is the greatest country in the world for producing athletes. Only underdevelopment in our soccer programs has kept us from competing with and beating the other countries in the world. The indoor game may alleviate the problem players have getting into and staying in shape—at least until the tradition of outdoor soccer has become more ingrained in our athletic consciousness.

Also, amateur coaches in areas where winter makes outdoor soccer impossible will find that indoor soccer is the answer to keeping players involved in the sport year-round. I am certain coaches will find improvement in passing and other skills after the competition of an indoor program. Players become more confident with the ball and understand the utilization of space much better. And the American player must learn to play in tight spaces and against tight marking if he is to succeed on a higher level. Indoor soccer provides this, as well as giving the players a new challenge.

HOW TO PLAY INDOOR SOCCER

Indoor soccer is played with a reduced team on a hockey rink. NASL uses six players—five field players and a goalkeeper. Although we play two or three defenders, they must be able to attack too, the same as in basketball and hockey. To turn a hockey rink into an indoor soccer field, an Astroturf rug is placed above an

This panoramic view of the Atoms/Russian Army Soccer match shows the hockey rink-sized playing field with its Astroturf floor covering.

insulation surface on top of the ice, and special soccer goals, reduced in size, are installed at either end of the arena.

Indoor soccer has not only adopted a hockey rink as playing surface but some hockey rules as well, which makes it even faster and more exciting. Because of the surrounding hockey boards, the ball is constantly in play, and the walls are used extensively in passing and shooting. Also, players can be substituted while the game is in progress.

In fact, practically the only times play stops is when goals are scored or when the referee detects some kind of foul play. Borrowing another leaf from the hockey rule book, an offending player is given a time penalty and the team plays a man short. Many soccer fans have written to our club to suggest that the time penalty system be incorporated into outdoor soccer play as well.

Because of the limited space—which requires many sharp turns, stops, and starts—and the limited number of breaks, indoor soccer players acquire a high degree of fitness. And, because contact between players is increased, they learn to play more carefully. Long passing and reckless clearing of the ball are nil; a player who clears a ball out of defense and kicks it into the spectators receives a two-minute penalty for delay of game, according to NASL rules. This results in a much more skillful and attractive soccer style, as well as constant action throughout the three 20-minute periods.

There is also a lot of goal-mouth action and many shots on goal in indoor soccer. Goal possibilities are increased partly by the number of rebound shots, for any shot that misses the goal or goes over the top immediately rebounds into play. In the experimental games in the NASL, quite a few of the goals were scored on such rebounds. The more the Atoms played, the more aware of the rebounds and the better able to use them (and defend against them) they became. So, in spite of the reduced size of indoor soccer goals, scores are much higher, and usually every player except the goalkeeper gets into the scoring column.

COLLEGE AND AMATEUR LEAGUES

The colleges and amateur leagues usually play their tournaments in armories or gymnasiums. Their goals are generally 7 feet high, 1 foot lower than the regular goal, and 12 or 14 feet wide, which is considerably smaller than the outdoor goal. They hold annual tournaments with as many as 16 teams competing in abbreviated games for a championship trophy. These tournaments have been growing in popularity during the past 5 years and have become a great way for the college and amateur players to stay in shape during their off season. When I coached in the college ranks, I found that indoor amateur soccer sharpened up the players' skills and shooting ability and kept them involved in the game.

127

INDOOR SOCCER STARS

Already indoor soccer is beginning to produce some really fine players. Paul Child, the San Jose Earthquakes' star forward and the NASL leading goal scorer for 1974, is a tremendous indoor player; he is very quick over short distances and can knock goals in from almost impossible angles. Jorge Siega, the New York Cosmos' outstanding left winger, is also a fantastic indoor player because of great dribbling ability and tight ball control; he learned his indoor soccer in Brazil where a type of indoor soccer is very popular among Brazilian players. And in England, every year, the first division professional players pit themselves against each other in a five-sided indoor soccer tournament in London; the players I have talked to enjoy this tournament very much and look forward to playing in it.

CONCLUSION

But whether you play soccer indoors or outdoors, the game is one of the most challenging physically and mentally. Someone said of soccer that it was like playing chess with no time to think about decisions. Can you even imagine hitting a difficult golf shot while running or being harassed by an opponent harassing you. Both as a player and a coach, I have found soccer to be the most demanding of games. It is a skill game, a contact sport, an endurance contest and a thinking man's game, all in one. In addition, soccer is rapidly becoming established in the American sports scene, and colleges and high schools are developing tremendous programs and followings for soccer. This gives the young player many more opportunities than he formerly had.

I hope that you derive as many rewards and thrills from the game as I have. Soccer is definitely a game for all sizes and shapes; it is inexpensive and provides a fine competitive atmosphere for every player.

glossary

BACKS: Defenders

BREAKAWAY: A situation in which the ball is clear of a team's defense and directly threatens their goal.

CENTER: A long kick from the side of the field to the center, usually in front of the goal (cross).

CENTER CIRCLE: A ten-yard-radius circle in the center of the field.

CHARGE: To push the opponent off balance legally by shoulder to shoulder contact.

CORNER KICK: A direct free kick taken by the offensive team from within the one-yard arc at the corner of the field.

COVER: To position oneself behind a teammate who is challenging an opponent for the ball so that if he is beaten you are there to defend.

CROSS: To kick the ball from near the touchline in front of the goal or across the field to a teammate.

DEAD BALL: A ball not in play, (which occurs when the ball passes out of the field of play, after a goal, after an infraction of the rules, or when play is stopped by the referees).

DEFENDER: A primarily defensive player who assists the goalkeeper in protecting the goal.

DIRECT FREE KICK: A dead ball kick that can score if it goes directly into the goal.

DROP BALL: A means of putting the ball into play by the referee after a temporary suspension of play not specifically covered in the rules.

FEINT: A deceptive movement by a player to fake an opponent.

FORWARD: A primarily attacking player whose responsibility is to create and score goals.

GOAL AREA: The area immediately in front of the goal enclosed by connected lines drawn six yards into the field from points on the goal line six yards toward the sidelines from the goal uprights.

GOALKEEPER: The last line of defense and the only player who can use his hands within the field of play; he is limited to using his hands only within the penalty area.

GOAL KICK: An indirect kick taken by the defensive team from any point within that half of the goal area nearest to where the ball crossed over the goal line.

GOAL LINE: The boundary line marking the end of the field.

HALF-VOLLEY: A kick of the ball just as it is rebounding off the ground.

HALFWAY LINE: A straight line connecting the two sidelines at the midfield and dividing the field into two equal parts.

HANDS: To touch the ball intentionally with any part of your hands or arms.

HOLDING: To obstruct an opponent's movement with your hands or arms.

INDIRECT FREE KICK: A dead ball from which a goal cannot be scored unless the ball has been touched or played by another player before entering the goal.

KICK-OFF: An indirect free kick from the center point of the field used as a means of starting play at the beginning of each period or restarting play after a goal has been scored.

LEAD: To pass the ball ahead of the receiver.

LINKMAN: Another name for midfielder.

LOB: A high, soft kick taken on the volley that lifts the ball over the heads of the opponents.

MARKING: Guarding an opponent. Man-to-man defending.

MIDFIELDER: An offensive *and* defensive player who is primarily responsible for linking the forwards and defenders.

OBSTRUCTING: Preventing the opponent from going around a player by standing in his path.

OFFSIDE: A player who is nearer to his opponent's goal than to the ball at the moment the ball is played, except in specific instances covered in the laws.

OVERLAP: The attacking play of a defender going down the touchline past his own winger.

PENALTY AREA: The area in front of the goal enclosed by connected lines drawn eighteen yards into the field from points on

130

the goal line eighteen yards toward the sidelines from the goal uprights.

PENALTY KICK: A direct free kick taken from the penalty kick mark.

PENALTY KICK MARK: A spot 12 yards from the midpoint of the goal line directly in front of the goal.

PITCH: Another name for the field of play.

PUNT: To kick the ball as it is dropped from the hands (used only by the goalkeeper).

SAVE: The prevention of an attempted goal by the goalkeeper by catching or deflecting the ball away from the goal.

SCORE: When the ball has passed completely over the goal line between the uprights and under the crossbar (one point).

SCREEN: To retain possession of and protect the ball by keeping your body between the ball and the opponent.

SHOT: A kick or head toward the goal in an attempt to score.

SLIDING TACKLE: An attempt to tackle the ball away from the opponent by sliding on the ground.

STRIKER: A central forward position in the team with a major responsibility for scoring goals.

SWEEPER: A defender who roams behind the fullback line to pick up passes and cover defense.

SWITCH: When two players intentionally exchange positions.

TACKLE: A move to take the ball away from an opponent when both players are playing the ball with their feet.

THROUGH-PASS: A pass to a point behind the defensive players, by kicking between them or over their heads.

THROW-IN: The method of restarting play after the ball has passed out of play across the touch lines.

TOUCHLINE: Sideline.

VOLLEY: Kicking the ball while it is in flight.

WALL PASS: A pass to a teammate followed by a first-time return pass for you to collect on the other side of the opponent (give and go).

WING: An area of the field near the touchline.

WINGER: The right or left forward who plays wide (near the touchline).

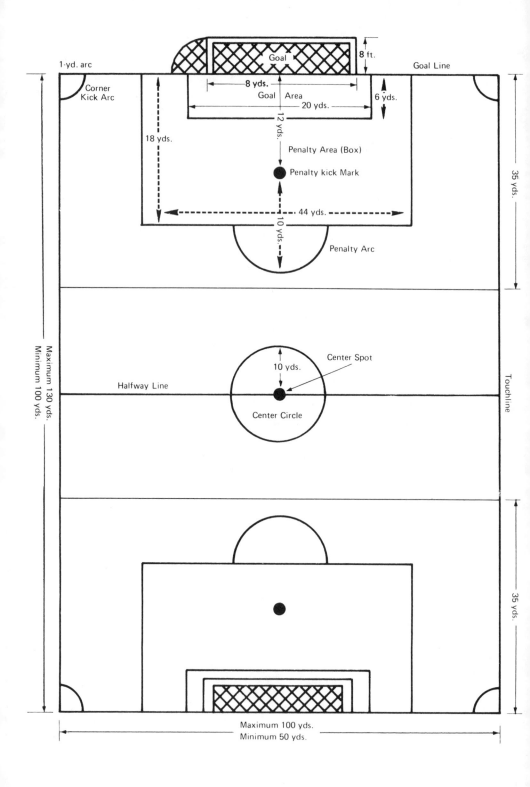

appendix A

condensed laws of soccer

The laws of the game of soccer are determined by FIFA in every country in the world. All players and teams associated with national soccer associations are using the FIFA regulated laws of the game in some form.

There are 17 laws, and they have been translated into many languages. Although the laws differ in detail, interpretation of these basic rules remains very much the same throughout the world.

This is partly because they are quite logical. When a group of boys organize a pickup game in the backyard, they begin by marking off the field, marking off the goals, selecting the ball for the game, and then picking up the sides. If you examine the first three laws of the game you will find that number one is the field of play; number two is the ball; and number three is the players. The rest of the laws follow as naturally as the first three. They have arisen in response to multitudes of interesting situations that have occurred in the course of play and require clear control. As I see it, the laws of the game serve a threefold purpose. They standardize the game by standardizing the field of play, the ball, the players' equipment, referees, etc; they keep the game moving with a spirit of competitiveness and fair play; and they penalize foul play and any unsportsmanlike conduct. The following is a brief descriptive discussion of each law.

LAW I: THE FIELD OF PLAY

The maximum length of the field allowed is 130 yards and the minimum length is 100 yards. The maximum width is 100 yards and the minimum width is 50 yards. The lines of the field used for marking off certain areas may not exceed 5 inches in width. A 5-foot-high post with a flag on top must be placed at each corner. At each

133

end of the field, two lines should be drawn at right angles to the goal line, 6 yards from each goal post. These will extend into the field of play for a distance of 6 yards and shall be joined by a line parallel with the goal line. This is called the goal area. At each end of the field, two lines shall be drawn at right angles to the goal line 18 yards from each goal post. These shall then extend into the field of play for a distance of 18 yards and shall be joined by a line parallel with the goal line. The enclosed area is known as the penalty area. At each corner flag, a quarter circle with a radius of one yard shall be drawn inside the field of play. The goal shall be placed on the center of each goal line at the ends of the field and shall consist of two upright posts 8 feet high joined by a horizontal crossbar which shall be 24 feet long. Therefore, a soccer goal is 8 feet high and 8 yards wide. Nets should be attached to the posts and crossbar and ground behind the goals so that any ball that goes into the goal will be caught in the net and the referee and players will know whether it went inside the goal or outside.

LAW II: THE BALL

The ball shall be spherical with the outer casing made of leather or other approved materials. The circumference of the ball cannot be more than 28 inches and not less than 27 inches. The weight of the ball at the start of the game shall not be more than 16 ounces nor less than 14 ounces.

LAW III: NUMBER OF PLAYERS

A game shall be played by two teams each consisting of not more than 11 players, one of whom shall be the goalkeeper. In the North American Soccer League, two substitutes shall be permitted. (It should be noted that this is a league decision rather than a FIFA law.) Any of the other players on the field may change places with the goalkeeper provided that the referee is informed before the change is made and that the change is made during a stoppage in the game.

LAW IV: PLAYERS' EQUIPMENT

Basically, this law requires player equipment which will not be dangerous to another player. The most dangerous piece of equipment generally is the footwear or the shoes. There are many types of screw-in studs that are made for soccer shoes, but to be legal studs must be made of leather, rubber, aluminum, or plastic. They cannot be longer than one-fourth inch, they cannot be less than one-half inch in diameter, and they must be round and must have a flat surface at the bottom. The referee goes to each dressing room prior to the game and checks each player's shoes.

The goalkeeper must wear colors that distinguish him from other players and the referees. Generally, the goalkeeper will wear the same color socks and shorts as the rest of his team but will wear a different color jersey. The common colors for goalkeepers' jerseys are green, red, and black. However, any contrasting color or design can be used by the goalkeeper.

LAW V: THE REFEREE

There is only one referee, and he is in complete charge of enforcing the laws of the game from the moment he enters the field of play. He is empowered to enforce the laws, keep a record of the game, and to act as a timekeeper. Also, he has discretionary power to stop the game for any infraction of the law or to suspend or terminate the game whenever elements, interference by spectators, or other causes necessitate such stoppage. He will caution any player guilty of misconduct or ungentlemanly behavior and suspend him from further participation in the game if his misconduct continues. He will allow no person other than the players and linesmen to enter the field of play without his permission. If, in his opinion, a player has been seriously injured, he will stop the game to have the player removed from the field of play and then resume the game. He will send off the field of play any player who, in his opinion, is guilty of violent conduct, serious foul play or the use of foul or abusive language.

135

LAW VI: THE LINESMEN

Two linesmen shall be appointed to each game. Their duty, subject to the decision of the referee, shall be to indicate when the ball is out of play and which side is entitled to the corner kick, goal kick or throw-in. They also signal when players are in an offside position or if a goal is scored. They shall also assist the referee to control the game in accordance with the laws. The linesmen will be equipped with flags, which are used as signaling devices to the referee. The linesmen will not enter the field of play and one will be placed on either side of the field.

LAW VII: DURATION OF THE GAME

The duration of the game shall be two equal periods of 45 minutes unless otherwise mutually agreed upon prior to the start of the game. In youth games, the normal playing time is two 30-minute halves.

LAW VIII: THE START OF PLAY

At the beginning of the game, choice of ends and the kick-off shall be decided by a toss of the coin by the referee and the two captains. The team winning the toss shall have the option of choice of ends or the kickoff. (Generally the captain winning the toss will select the choice of ends. His decision will be dictated by wind, sun, field conditions, or perhaps a team superstition.) The referee gives a signal and the game starts by a player taking a place kick into his opponents' half of the field of play. Every player shall be in his own half of the field and every player of the team opposing that of the kicker shall remain not less than 10 yards from the ball until it is kicked off. On the kickoff, the ball must travel the distance of its own circumference before the game is officially started. The kicker shall not play the ball a second time until it has been touched or played by one of the players on the opposing side. After a goal has been scored, the game shall be restarted in like manner by a player of the team losing the ball. After half time, ends shall be changed and the kickoff shall be taken by a player of the opposite team than that of the player who started the game. A goal cannot be scored directly from a kickoff.

LAW IX: BALL IN AND OUT OF PLAY

The ball is out of play when (a) it has wholly crossed the goal line or touchline whether on the ground or in the air, (b) the game has been stopped by the referee. It should be noted that unlike other American sports, the ball must go completely over the line before it is out of play.

LAW X: METHOD OF SCORING

A goal is scored when the whole of the ball has passed over the goal line between the goal posts and under the crossbar, provided that it has not been thrown, carried or propelled by hand or arm by a player of the attacking side except in the case of a goalkeeper who is within his own penalty area. The team scoring the greater number of goals during a game shall be the winner.

LAW XI: OFFSIDE

This law is perhaps the most difficult to interpret and to understand. Many decisions are made by the referee on the field utilizing the help of his linesmen that players within the game do not understand or spectators see in other ways. In actual fact, the offside law is fairly simple if you understand the following:

A player is offside if he is nearer his opponents' goal line than the ball at the moment the ball is played unless (a) he is in his own half of the field of play, (b) there are two of his opponents nearer to his own goal line than he is, (c) the ball last touched an opponent or was last played by him, (d) he receives the ball direct from a goal kick, a corner kick, a throw in, or when it was dropped by the referee, or (e) he is behind the ball.

You can never be offside if you are in your own half of the field. In 1973 the North American Soccer League introduced a "blue line" concept in which a line is drawn across the field 35 yards from each goal line. Now, your own half of the field of play is the regular half, plus the distance to the 35-yard offside line. Only from the 35-yard line to the goal can a player be in an offside position.

Also, you can never be offsides if there are two or more opponents nearer to the goal line than you are. In most cases, the opposing goalkeeper is one of the two opponents. Therefore, one other opponent must be between you and the goal or you are in an offside position.

LAW XII: FOULS AND MISCONDUCT

This law is the referee's guide to maintaining discipline on the field at all times by not allowing any member on the field to gain an advantage while the game is in progress. There are nine fouls for which a referee must penalize a player: (1) kicking or attempting to kick an opponent, (2) tripping an opponent, (3) jumping at an opponent, (4) charging an opponent in a violent or dangerous manner, (5) charging an opponent from behind unless the player is obstructing the ball, (6) striking or attempting to strike an opponent, (7) holding an opponent with his hands or any part of his arm, (8) pushing an opponent with his hands or any part of his arm, (9) touching the ball with his hand, carrying, striking or propelling the ball with his hand. For any of these fouls, the referee will award a direct free kick to the opposing side from the place where the offense occurred. If any of these fouls are committed by the defending side within the penalty area, a penalty kick will be awarded. Five other offenses result in an indirect free kick:

(1) Playing in a manner considered by the referee to be dangerous, e.g., attempting to kick the ball while it is held by the goalkeeper; raising the foot too high in attempting to kick the ball, which could be dangerous since one player might kick another player in the face; or, heading the ball in too low a position so that the heading player may get kicked in the face or head.

(2) Charging fairly but when the ball is not within playing distance of the player concerned and he is definitely not trying to play it.

(3) Intentionally obstructing an opponent when not playing the ball, e.g., a player running in front of an opponent who is chasing the ball to obstruct him from getting to the ball rather than trying to play the ball himself.

(4) Charging the goalkeeper—except when he is (a) holding the ball, (b) obstructing an opponent, (c) has passed outside his own goal area.

(5) When playing as goalkeeper (a) taking more than four steps while holding, bouncing, or throwing the ball in the air and catching it again without releasing it so that it is played by another player, or (b) indulging in tactics, which, in the opinion of the referee, are designed merely to hold up the game and thus waste time.

In order to maintain discipline on the field, a referee is empowered to caution a player for the following four offenses: (1) Entering or re-entering the field of play to join or re-join his team after the game has commenced or leaving the field of play during the progress of the game without, in either case, having received a signal from the referee showing him that he may do so; (2) persistently infringing on the laws of the game —for example, consistently fouling his opponents, in which case the referee should caution him; (3) showing by word or action dissent from any decision given by the referee; (4) being guilty of ungentlemanly conduct, such as foul language or any of the above offenses. In addition to the caution, an indirect free kick will be awarded to the opposing

139

side from the place where the offense occurred. When a caution is given to a player, a referee will hold up a yellow card and write down the player's number. The player, therefore, is playing under a caution and any continuation will result in his being sent off the field.

Three major reasons for sending a player off the field are (1) The player is guilty of violent conduct or serious foul play; (2) he uses foul or abusive language; (3) he persists in misconduct after having received a caution. In our laws, if a player is sent off the field he cannot re-enter the field and the team will play with 10 players instead of 11.

I am sure that you can recognize after reading the above laws of the game that there is no place for foul play or fighting. In almost every instance, a fight between two players will result in both of them being removed from the field of play and the game continuing with one less player on each side. Since it is urgent for the players to win on skill and tactics, coaches must discourage foul play and misbehavior.

LAW XIII: FREE KICK

A free kick will be classified as a direct free kick or an indirect free kick. In a direct free kick, a goal can be scored directly against the defending side. In other words, a player can strike a dead ball into the opponents' goal and the goal will be allowed. An indirect free kick cannot be scored unless the ball has been played or touched by a player other than the kicker before passing through the goal. As we have learned from LAW XII, the serious offenses result in a direct free kick, which is far more dangerous than an indirect free kick.

There are several things that you should know about both the direct and indirect free kicks: (a) Players from the opposing side must be a minimum of 10 yards from the ball before the free kick is taken; (b) when the free kick is taken, the kicker shall not play the ball a second time until it has been touched or played by another player; (c) the ball must be stationary when the free kick is taken; (d) the ball shall be in play when it has traveled the distance of its own circumference.

LAW XIV: PENALTY KICK

Any fouls which would result in a direct free kick that occur inside the penalty box will result in a penalty kick. All players except the goalkeeper and the player taking the penalty kick must line up outside the penalty box (and at least 10 yards from the ball, which is the reason for the arc at the edge of the penalty area). The goalkeeper must stand on his own goal line between his own goal posts until the ball is kicked. The player taking the kick must kick the ball forward, and he cannot play the ball a second time until it has been touched or played by another player. The penalty spot is 12 yards from the goal line. All penalty kicks shall be taken from the penalty spot and the ball shall be in play as soon as it has traveled the distance of its circumference, as in all other free kicks.

LAW XV: THE THROW-IN

When the entire ball passes over the touchline either on the ground or in the air, it shall be thrown in from the point where it crossed the line by a player of the team opposite to that of the player who last touched it. The thrower, at the moment of delivering the ball, must face the field of play, and part of each foot shall be either on the touchline or on the ground outside the touchline. The thrower shall use both hands and shall deliver the ball from behind and over his head. The ball shall be in play immediately once it enters the field of play, but the thrower cannot play the ball again until it has been touched or played by another player. A goal cannot be scored directly from a throw-in. If the ball is improperly thrown in, a throw-in shall be awarded to a player of the opposing team. Basically then, there are three things you should always remember on a throw-in: (a)

Keep both feet on the ground, (b) throw the ball with both hands, and (c) throw the ball from behind the head directly over the head.

LAW XVI: THE GOAL KICK

When the whole of the ball passes over the goal line (excluding that portion between the goal posts) either in the air or on the ground, having last been played by the attacking team, it will be kicked directly into play by a player of the defending team from the point within that half of the goal area nearest to where it crossed the line. Players on the opposing team shall remain outside the penalty area while the kick is being taken. If the ball does not go fully out of the penalty area, the kick shall be retaken. A goal cannot be scored directly from a goal kick.

LAW XVII: THE CORNER KICK

When the whole of the ball passes over the goal line (excluding that portion between the goal posts) either in the air or on the ground, having last been played by the defending team, a member of the attacking team shall take a corner kick. At each corner of the field, there is a quarter circle with a one-yard radius. The whole of the ball must be placed within the quarter circle. A corner flag post may not be removed and the kick must be taken from the quarter circle. A goal may be scored directly from a corner kick. Players of the opposing team must stay 10 yards away from the ball until it is kicked. The ball is in play once it has traveled its own circumference. And, as in all other free kicks, the kicker may not play the ball a second time until it has been touched or played by another player.

appendix B

NASL indoor soccer rules
(excluding violations)

GENERAL:

The rules which apply to NASL outdoor soccer shall also apply to indoor soccer, but with the following exceptions:

EXCEPTIONS:

LAW I—*Playing Area*

Approx. — 200' x 85'

Perimeter Wall — 3'6" x 4'6" high fully enclosing area.

Goal — 4' x 16' wide.

Goal Area — 18' wide x 5' from the goal line.

Penalty Area — 30' x 25'

Penalty Spot — 9" diam. x 24' from the center of goal line.

Penalty Spot Arc — 10' radius from penalty spot.

Corner Spot — 9" diam. at point of intersection of sideline and extention of the goal area line drawn 5' from the goal line.

Center Spot — 9" diam.

Center Circle — 10' radius.

Yellow Line — 30' from halfway line across field width, each half.

Markings — 3" min. 5" max. width.

Center Line — Indicated by a white line across field.

Side Lines — Broken line from corner spot to corner spot, on both sides of the field at a distance of 3' from the perimeter wall.

All areas include the line width. Ball must be total diameter over a line to be out of an area. If partially on or over a line it is still within the area.

Goal face is flush with perimeter wall and nets at least 4' rearward.

LAW II—*The Ball.* As used in the outdoor game.

LAW III—*Number of Players.* 14 per squad maximum.

Minimum per team on field at any time—4. Maximum—6. Time penalty is delayed if team would reduce below 4. One player must be a goalkeeper.

Substitutions. May occur on unlimited basis provided player leaving the field arrives at the bench before replacement enters field.

LAW IV—*Player's Equipment.* Sneaker type or multi-studded shoes. Goalkeeper must wear different color jersey from other outfield players'.

LAW V—*Referees.* The Referee has sole jurisdiction over the game. He is assisted by timekeepers and linesmen.

LAW VI—*Linesmen and Timekeepers.* Linesmen shall assist the referee to indicate yellow line and substitute violations and to indicate goals scored. Timekeepers shall operate the time and scoreboard details and the time penalties to ensure correct re-entry of players.

LAW VII—*Duration of the Game.* Three equal periods of 20 minutes, with two 15 minute intervals.

LAW VIII—*Start of Play.* Team Captains flip coin and winner elects to kick off or choose direction to attack in first period. Teams change direction at each interval.

LAW IX—*Ball in Play. Ball is Out* when it passes over the perimeter wall, a goal is scored, or when referee calls time out.

Ball is in Play at all other times, even if it rebounds from the referee, perimeter wall, goalpost, surrounding screens, etc.

LAW X—*Method of Scoring.* A goal is scored when the *Whole* of the ball passes completely over the goal line, provided no infraction of the law has been committed by the attacking team, or other incident covered by the law applies.

LAW XI—*Offside and Three Zone Pass Violation.* The outdoor offside law does not apply to indoor soccer.

Three Zone Pass. If the ball is passed forward by any member of the attacking team and it passes over two yellow lines without being touched by any other player (of either team), the pass shall be termed a three zone pass. If a player makes a three zone pass, the referee will award an Indirect Free Kick to the opposing team, to be taken at the point where the ball crossed the yellow line nearest to the goal being defended by the player making the pass. When any team is playing with two players fewer than the opponents then the three zone pass restriction shall not apply to the team that is depleted.

LAW XII—*Fouls and Misconduct.* The outdoor rules apply.

LAW XIII—*Free Kicks (Direct and Indirect).* The outdoor rules apply.

LAW XIV—*Penalty Kicks.* Penalty Kicks are those kicks taken from the penalty spot.

All players except the kicker and goalkeeper must be outside the penalty area and penalty area arc at the taking of this direct kick at goal. The kicker may not play the ball a second time unless it rebounds from goalkeeper. Penalty kicks are awarded for offenses committed by defenders against an attacker in the penalty area. BUT ONLY INTENTIONALLY NOT ACCIDENTALLY. The penalty offenses are:

1. Kicking (an opponent); 2. Tripping; 3. Striking; 4. Jumping (at opponent); 5. Pushing; 6. Holding; 7. Charging violently; 8. Charging in the back; 9. Handling the ball (by hand or arm from shoulder down, except goalkeeper).

LAW XV—*Throw-In.* In place of the throw-in used in regular soccer, the ball will be put back into play with an Indirect Free Kick with the ball being placed on the sideline at the point nearest to where the ball went out of play. This is termed then a kick-in instead of a throw-in. (If a player *deliberately* puts the ball out over the perimeter wall, he shall serve a *delay of game* time penalty.)

LAW XVI—*Goal Kick.* The outdoor rule applies.

LAW XVII—*Corner Kick.* The outdoor rule applies with the corner being taken from the corner spot.

NOTE: Any incident not covered by these laws shall be dealt with by the Referee at his discretion. Such incidents shall be referred back to the Commissioner so that an amendment to the rules can be made to cover any future such incident. The decision of the referee, insofar as the result of the game is concerned, is final.

index

147